The Munich Olympics

GREAT DISASTERS
REFORMS and RAMIFICATIONS

The Munich Olympics

Hal Marcovitz

CHELSEA HOUSE PUBLISHERS
Philadelphia

CHELSEA HOUSE PUBLISHERS

Editor in Chief Sally Cheney
Director of Production Kim Shinners
Creative Manager Takeshi Takahashi
Manufacturing Manager Diann Grasse

Staff for THE MUNICH OLYMPICS

Assistant Editor Susan Naab
Picture Researcher Sarah Bloom
Production Assistant Jaimie Winkler
Series Designer Takeshi Takahashi
Cover Designer: Keith Trego
Layout 21st Century Publishing and Communications, Inc.

First Printing

1 3 5 7 9 8 6 4 2

The Chelsea House World Wide Web address is
http://www.chelseahouse.com

Library of Congress Cataloging-in-Publication Data

Marcovitz, Hal.
   The Munich Olympics / by Hal Marcovitz.
      p. cm. — (Great disasters, reforms and ramifications)
Includes bibliographical references (p.   ) and index.
Summary: Provides an account of the terrorist attacks against
Israeli athletes during the 1972 Olympic games, profiling some
of the individuals involved and exploring the political and
historical reasons for the acts.
   ISBN 0-7910-6737-8 — ISBN 0-7910-6911-7 (pbk.)
   1. Olympic Games (20th : 1972 : Munich, Germany)—
Juvenile literature. 2. Terrorism—Germany (West)—Munich
—History—Juvenile literature. [1. Olympic Games (20th : 1972 :
Munich, Germany) 2. Terrorism. 3. Athletes.] I. Title. II. Series.
GV722 1972 .M394 2002
796.48—dc21   2001053813

Contents

GREAT DISASTERS
REFORMS and RAMIFICATIONS

Jill McCaffrey
National Chairman
Armed Forces Emergency Services
American Red Cross

Introduction

Disasters have always been a source of fascination and awe. Tales of a great flood that nearly wipes out all life are among humanity's oldest recorded stories, dating at least from the second millennium B.C., and they appear in cultures from the Middle East to the Arctic Circle to the southernmost tip of South America and the islands of Polynesia. Typically gods are at the center of these ancient disaster tales—which is perhaps not too surprising, given the fact that the tales originated during a time when human beings were at the mercy of natural forces they did not understand.

To a great extent, we still are at the mercy of nature, as anyone who reads the newspapers or watches nightly news broadcasts can attest.

Hurricanes, earthquakes, tornados, wildfires, and floods continue to exact a heavy toll in suffering and death, despite our considerable knowledge of the workings of the physical world. If science has offered only limited protection from the consequences of natural disasters, it has in no way diminished our fascination with them. Perhaps that's because the scale and power of natural disasters force us as individuals to confront our relatively insignificant place in the physical world and remind us of the fragility and transience of our lives. Perhaps it's because we can imagine ourselves in the midst of dire circumstances and wonder how we would respond. Perhaps it's because disasters seem to bring out the best and worst instincts of humanity: altruism and selfishness, courage and cowardice, generosity and greed.

As one of the national chairmen of the American Red Cross, a humanitarian organization that provides relief for victims of disasters, I have had the privilege of seeing some of humanity's best instincts. I have witnessed communities pulling together in the face of trauma; I have seen thousands of people answer the call to help total strangers in their time of need.

Of course, helping victims after a tragedy is not the only way, or even the best way, to deal with disaster. In many cases planning and preparation can minimize damage and loss of life—or even avoid a disaster entirely. For, as history repeatedly shows, many disasters are caused not by nature but by human folly, shortsightedness, and unethical conduct. For example, when a land developer wanted to create a lake for his exclusive resort club in Pennsylvania's Allegheny Mountains in 1880, he ignored expert warnings and cut corners in reconstructing an earthen dam. On May 31, 1889, the dam gave way, unleashing 20 million tons of water on the towns below. The Johnstown Flood, the deadliest in American history, claimed more than 2,200 lives. Greed and negligence would figure prominently in the Triangle Shirtwaist Company fire in 1911. Deplorable conditions in the garment sweatshop, along with a failure to give any thought to the safety of workers, led to the tragic deaths of 146 persons. Technology outstripped wisdom only a year later, when the designers of the luxury liner *Titanic* smugly declared their state-of-the-art ship "unsinkable," seeing no need to provide lifeboat capacity for everyone onboard. On the night of April 14, 1912, more than 1,500 passengers and crew paid for this hubris with their lives after the ship collided with an iceberg and sank. But human catastrophes aren't always the unforeseen consequences of carelessness or folly. In the 1940s the leaders of Nazi Germany purposefully and systematically set out to exterminate all Jews, along with Gypsies, homosexuals, the mentally ill, and other so-called undesirables. More recently terrorists have targeted random members of society, blowing up airplanes and buildings in an effort to advance their political agendas.

The books in the GREAT DISASTERS: REFORMS AND RAMIFICATIONS series examine these and other famous disasters, natural and human made. They explain the causes of the disasters, describe in detail how events unfolded, and paint vivid portraits of the people caught up in dangerous circumstances. But these books are more than just accounts of what happened to whom and why. For they place the disasters in historical perspective, showing how people's attitudes and actions changed and detailing the steps society took in the wake of each calamity. And in the end, the most important lesson we can learn from any disaster—as well as the most fitting tribute to those who suffered and died—is how to avoid a repeat in the future.

Munich, Germany hosted the 1972 Summer Olympics, in part to show off to the world the peaceful, model society of a "New Germany." The modern, friendly atmosphere symbolized a complete reversal of the horror of the former Nazi government.

The Sabra

Moshe Weinberg sat in a theater in Munich, Germany, watching his friend, actor Shmuel Rodensky, play the role of Tevye in *Fiddler on the Roof.*

The play tells the story of a simple Jewish milkman in czarist Russia trying to hold onto old traditions while the world changes around him. It is a heart-warming story with rousing music and hilarious moments of comedy.

Years ago, it would have been unthinkable for a play such as *Fiddler on the Roof* to be presented on a stage in Germany. During the regime of Adolf Hitler and the Nazi party, Jews throughout Europe were targeted for extermination. In the 1930s and 1940s, they were forced out of their homes and shipped to concentration camps, where they were made to perform slave labor or sent to their deaths in gas chambers. More than 6,000,000 Jews died in what has come to be known as the "Holocaust."

Hitler's regime, known as the "Third Reich," fell at the end of World War II. Nazi criminals were tried and executed. Many of the Jews who survived the camps made their way to the Middle East, where they helped found the new state, or country, of Israel.

Moshe Weinberg was an Israeli, but unlike many of his countrymen he was a "sabra," a native-born Israeli. He was born in 1939 in the then-British colony of Palestine. In 1948, when the United Nations recognized Israel as an independent nation, Weinberg became an Israeli citizen.

In Hebrew—the official language of Israel—sabra stems from the word for cactus. Israeli citizens born in Palestine prior to the declaration of statehood are thought to be similar to the cactus—they are prickly on the outside but sweet on the inside.

That description fit Weinberg perfectly. He was naturally athletic and excelled in wrestling. In 1965, he won a gold medal in freestyle wrestling at the Macabee Games, a quadrennial competition held in Israel to which the world's best Jewish athletes are invited. At home in Tel Aviv, one of Israel's largest cities, Weinberg worked as a physical education teacher and coach. In fact, he had traveled to Munich to coach his country's wrestlers who were competing in the 1972 Olympic Games.

In early August, just weeks before the Munich Games were set to begin, French wrestler Daniel Robin went to Tel Aviv at Weinberg's invitation to test the Israeli wrestlers and help Weinberg decide whom to select for the Olympic team. Robin was a former world champion who won two silver medals at the 1968 Olympics in Mexico City.

Robin stayed in Weinberg's Tel Aviv home. Weinberg had married the year before and on August 3, the day Robin arrived in Tel Aviv, Weinberg's wife Miriam gave birth to a boy, whom the couple named Gur.

"Moshe was beside himself with joy," Robin recalled. "He overflowed with vitality and kindness. But, during that evening, I noticed him with a faraway, almost sad, look. I wondered aloud whether anything was wrong, and he forced himself to laugh, and said, 'Nothing at all! It was just, you see, that I was wondering whether my son, Gur, one day, would know what peace is."

Peace meant a lot to Weinberg because he had worked hard and risked his life to make Israel's borders secure against its enemies, the Arab states of the Middle East. For 11 years, Weinberg served in his country's military, the Israel Defense Force. All young Israeli men and women are required to serve in the military—it is regarded not only as their patriotic duty to defend their nation, but their moral duty to protect their fellow Jews from the type of aggression launched by the Nazis. As for Weinberg, he was more than just a foot soldier in the Israeli army; indeed, he had served in an elite squad of commandos assigned to risky missions that required great courage, cunning, and physical skills.

But on this night in Munich, thoughts of his days in the military were well behind him. Weinberg sat in the theater with several representatives from the team, including Esther Shahamorov, a sprinter-hurdler, and Amitzur Shapira, a track coach. The Olympics had been going well for Shahamorov—she was advancing through the competition and hoped to make the finals in her event, the 100-meter hurdles.

The actors spoke their lines in German, which few of the Israelis understood. But Shapira was fluent in Yiddish—a language similar to German that had been

Different religions and ethnicities were recognized, even celebrated, in Germany in 1972. *Fiddler on the Roof*, a play about Russian Jews, could now be openly performed and attended. The Israeli Olympic team attended such a performance the night before the September 5th tragedy.

spoken for centuries by European Jews—and he was able to translate the dialogue for his teammates.

"We felt great; it was a wonderful experience," recalled Shahamorov. "I had reached the second stage, and it felt like the whole delegation had won. Everybody celebrated in the success. It was a very moving night. In the middle of the play we were invited to have a glass of wine. They took photos of me and Shmuel Rodensky. They lifted us in the air, the whole delegation."

After the performance, some of the Israelis returned to their rooms in the Olympic Village. Weinberg decided to spend time with Rodensky, and the two men had dinner together in a Munich restaurant. After dinner, the wrestling coach and actor wandered through Munich's nightclub district, reveling in the experience of being together during a special time in their lives.

By now, it was the early morning hours of September 5. Later that day, Weinberg expected to accompany Mark Slavin, one of the team's wrestlers, to his competition. Weinberg and Rodensky parted company, and Weinberg made his way to the Olympic Village where he found the gate locked. Athletes and coaches returning to their apartments after a late night in Munich's entertainment district usually came back to locked gates since the Games had commenced 11 days before. And so, to gain entrance to the Village, they simply hopped over the chain-link fence. Their actions were always met with a wink from the Munich policemen assigned to patrol the Olympic Village.

The German authorities were fearful that memories of their country's authoritarian past would be conjured up by a threatening police presence so they ordered their policemen to maintain low profiles during the Games. Instead of police uniforms, the officers wore blue blazers. They carried no guns, and were armed with only walkie-talkies to summon help.

Weinberg easily scaled the fence and found his way to Number 31 Connollystrasse—the Olympic Village building with four apartments designated for the Israeli team. He made his way up the stairs to Apartment One and went to sleep.

Soon, he would be roused from bed.

The Games of Peace and Joy

Venues for the Summer Games in Munich, named "The Games of Peace and Joy," being constructed in February 1972. The Olympics are an opportunity to put aside nationality and politics, and pit individual athlete against athlete in honor of the original Olympic events first held in Greece in 776 B.C.

2

The Greek team arrived first, marching into Olympic Stadium to the roaring approval of more than 80,000 spectators. As each country filed in behind the Greeks, fans who made the trek to Munich for the 20th Olympiad cheered wildly. Many waved tiny flags from their home countries to show their national pride as well as a fellowship with the world's citizens, come together for this most joyful of athletic competitions. Outside the stadium, an international television audience of more than a billion people watched the opening ceremonies unfold.

The Summer Olympics are held every four years, and nations vie in a vigorous competition to host the Games. The German government had lobbied hard for the Olympics, hoping to introduce its country to the world as a modern and peace-loving nation that had wiped out the horrors of its Nazi past. In fact, the last time the Olympics had been staged in Germany was in 1936. Adolf Hitler intended the Games to be a propaganda vehicle for Nazism, showing the athletic superiority of the German race. But his plans were largely thwarted by Jesse Owens, a black American track-and-field star who set world and Olympic records in several events.

But now, on August 26, 1972, as the Greek team entered the stadium for what the German Olympic Committee had labeled "The Games of Peace and Joy," it appeared as though the world was willing to forgive the Germans and welcome them into the community of nations.

"The first thing you felt on arriving in Munich was the utter determination of the Germans, whether they be Olympic officials, policemen, journalists, or indeed the general population of Munich, to wipe out the past," recalled British TV reporter Gerald Seymour. "We were totally overwhelmed by the sense that this was the new Germany. It was a massive attempt, and it hit you straight away, by the Germans to appear open and modern and shorn of their past. Friendliness was in overdrive."

Indeed, the Germans had spared no expense in preparing Munich for the Games. Munich is an old city in the German state of Bavaria that dates back to the 12th century. The original gates to the city, built in 1310, are still standing today. Among the landmarks a visitor to Munich would find are the Frauenkirche, a church built in 1468 with a stone tower that stands nearly 300 feet high; the Marienplatz, which is the sprawling public square in the center of the city, and Theatiner Church, which was erected in 1690 and features a copper dome more than 100 feet high. Munich is also the location of Bayerische Motoren Werke—the BMW automobile company, one of the largest corporations in Europe.

Truly, Munich is one of Europe's most historic and colorful cities.

But Munich has also earned a black mark in history. In the 1920s, Hitler regarded Munich as his home and planted the seeds for the Nazi party in the city's beer halls. In 1938, Hitler, by then the dictator of Germany, forced European leaders to sign a treaty in Munich that turned part of what is now the Czech Republic over to Germany. That treaty was an early step toward Hitler's plans to conquer Europe and it led to the outbreak of World War II.

When the Germans won the right to host the 1972 Olympics, they aimed to turn Munich into a modern showplace for the "New Germany."

The crown jewel of their plans was Olympic Stadium —the 80,000-seat main venue for the Games that cost more than $60 million—an incredible amount in 1966, the year construction started. The stadium was erected under a sprawling, tent-like roof that stunned the world-wide architectural community by its radical design.

Elsewhere, the Germans built arenas, gymnasiums, and swimming pools to serve as sites for the competitions, as well as dozens of apartment buildings to house the athletes.

"I don't have words to express how beautiful this place is," remarked Colombian athlete Diego Hanao, after he first entered the Olympic Village.

■   ■   ■

In the Olympic opening ceremony, it is traditional for the Greeks to lead the parade of nations because the concept of the Games originated in their country in the year 776 B.C. The modern Olympic Games, in which countries send their best athletes to a host nation for a series of competitions, started in 1896.

Following the entrance of the Greek team, the other nations filed into Olympic Stadium in alphabetical order—Egypt was first to follow the Greeks, because in German the word Egypt is spelled "Aegypt." Next to enter was Afghanistan, followed by Albania, Brazil and so on. Each team was preceded by an athlete carrying the country's flag. When the parade finally concluded, some 7,000 athletes representing 121 countries had marched into the stadium.

The largest teams were sent by the largest countries. The United States sent 420 athletes to Munich. Among them was swimmer Mark Spitz, who would soon capture the world's attention with his dazzling speed and endurance. Spitz would go on to win seven gold medals at the Munich Olympics—a record that stands today.

A large contingent of athletes was also sent by the Soviet Union, the massive country that dominated the communist world after the end of World War II. Marching in the ranks of the Soviet athletes was a tiny female gymnast, 17-year-old Olga Korbut, whose incandescent, gravity-defying performances in the competition would revolutionize her sport and make her an international celebrity.

Not all nations arrived at the Olympics expecting to win medals or set records. Israel, for example, sent a team to Munich that included just 13 athletes as well as five coaches and referees. Only Esther Shahamorov was given a chance to win a medal. Still, the Israeli team marched proudly into Olympic Stadium, its blue-and-white flag displaying the six-pointed Star of David—the symbol of the Jewish religion—held aloft by marksman Henry Herskowitz.

Soon, the procession of athletes was over and the entertainment portion of the opening ceremony commenced. A parade of 3,200 German boys and girls dressed

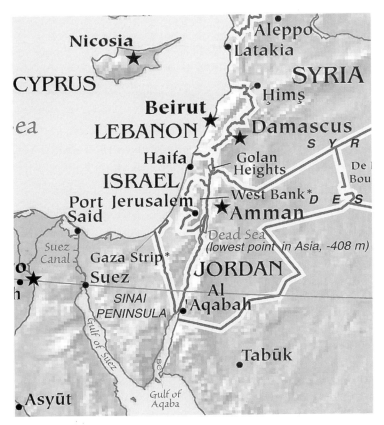

Israel, previously a British colony, won its independence and was designated an official Jewish state and homeland in 1948. Any Jews from around the world could become recognized citizens under the Law of Return.

in blue frocks and yellow shorts filled the running track, where they presented a grand maypole dance. Next, 40 Bavarian folk dancers dressed in traditional costumes entertained the athletes and fans with an electric performance featuring cracking bullwhips. And then, 5,000 doves were released into the blue sky over Munich, symbolizing the desire by the Germans to host an event whose theme would be peace.

In the weeks preceding the Olympics, it appeared the Games would get off to a rocky start. Twenty-seven African nations threatened to boycott the Games unless Rhodesia was banned from the competition. Now known as Zimbabwe, the nation practiced apartheid in 1972 and was ruled by a white minority government. When black athletes from America and other countries also threatened to boycott, the International Olympic Committee relented and excluded Rhodesia from the Games.

Finally, a runner entered the stadium carrying the Olympic torch. Months before, the torch started its journey to Munich from Peloponnese in Greece, the site of the first Olympiad. Now, Gunter Zahn, an 18-year-old member of the German track-and-field team, entered the stadium holding the torch aloft. Zahn circled the oval running track and ascended the stadium stairs to light the Olympic beacon.

"I declare open the Olympic Games celebrating the 20th Olympiad of the modern era," proclaimed German President Gustav Heinemann.

For the next two weeks, nations that were bitter enemies would compete against one another not with guns and missiles, but with track shoes, basketballs, and boxing gloves. There was no question, though, that outside Munich tensions were on edge in many parts of the world. One such place was the Middle East, where Israel and its Jewish citizens were surrounded by hostile Arab neighbors.

■   ■   ■

Israelis had been fighting with their Arab neighbors even before Israel was recognized as a nation. Fighting broke out between Jewish settlers and Arab armies from Egypt, Syria, Jordan, Iraq, Saudi Arabia, and Lebanon in November 1947, shortly after the United Nations announced the new borders of Israel. For centuries, Palestinian Arabs of the Middle East also regarded the territory as their homeland. Palestinians and their supporters in the Arab nations insisted the land belonged to the Palestinians, not the Jews.

"All our efforts to find a peaceful solution to the

Palestinian problem have failed," said King Abdullah of Jordan. "The only way left for us is war. I will have the pleasure and honor to save Palestine."

The conflict became known as the Israeli "War of Independence."

The first large-scale assault occurred on January 9, 1948, when an army of 1,000 Arab soldiers attacked Jewish settlements in the north. The British, who were still in control of the colony at that point, admitted they could do little to stem the onslaught, and they left the fighting to the Jews.

The Jews fought hard and won many battles. But they lost some, too. On May 6, 1948, an Arab army attacked a Jewish settlement at Kfar Etzion, massacring the defenders.

Still, Israeli leaders proceeded with their plans to create their own state. Independence was declared on May 14, 1948. The British turned over the country to the

Cabinet Ministers celebrate the beginning of the new government on Israeli Independence Day, 1948, by singing the national anthem during a ceremony. A Swedish diplomat incorrectly surmised, "The Palestinian Arabs had at present no will of their own." Therefore, a separate Arab state was not needed.

new Israeli citizens, further infuriating the Arabs.

"This will be a war of extermination and a momentous massacre which will be spoken of like the Mongolian massacres and the Crusades," declared Azzam Pasha, Secretary-General of the Arab League, the loose confederation of the Middle East Arab states.

Pasha's prediction turned out to be a hollow threat. The Arabs were poorly armed and poorly trained, and they lacked the will to fight. This was years before Arab leaders gained control of their countries' vast oil reserves from western oil companies, a circumstance that today has given the Arab countries incredible wealth with which to buy weapons and train soldiers. But in the 1940s, the Arab armies were unable to defeat even the ragtag Israeli defenders. A truce was declared on June 11, 1948, although sporadic fighting occasionally broke out through 1949.

The Arab nations grudgingly agreed to observe Israel's borders and an uneasy peace fell over the Middle East. As for the Palestinians, they had no place to go. Many of them became refugees, forced to live in camps in Jordan and other Arab countries.

"The Palestinian Arabs had at present no will of their own," wrote Swedish diplomat Folke Bernadotte, who helped negotiate the 1948 cease-fire. "Neither have they ever developed any specifically Palestinian nationalism. The demand for a separate Arab state in Palestine is consequently weak. It would seem as though in existing circumstances most of the Palestinian Arabs would be quite content to be incorporated in (Jordan)."

The Israelis celebrated their independence and started the job of building cities. Over the years, though, they found themselves defending their territory against increasingly bold strikes by their Arab neighbors. Egyptian President Gamal Abdel Nasser, who came to

Surrounded by hostile Arab nations, Israel has continuously had to defend its borders of desert sand against would-be invaders. Brigadier General Ariel Sharon and Prime Minister Menachem Begin took part in the Six-Day War of 1967, considered a major victory for the young country.

power after the truce was declared, had resolved to destroy Israel. Other Arab leaders made similar vows.

Finally, in 1967, Israel reacted to a military buildup along its borders by launching attacks against Egypt, Syria, and Jordan. Indeed, the Israeli army attacked with such ferocity that it shocked the larger Arab forces, easily routing its enemies. The conflict was over in six days and, in fact, came to be known as the Six-Day War. The Israeli people regarded the victory over the Arabs as the greatest moment in their young country's history.

As a result of the war, each of the Arab states lost territory to Israel. In Jordan, that territory included the West Bank of the Jordan River, a region Palestinian Arabs especially regarded as their homeland. Following the war, the West Bank came under the control of Israeli soldiers, who maintained it as a buffer zone between Israel and the Jewish state's enemies in Jordan.

Palestinians in the West Bank grew to hate their Israeli occupiers. Many of them were forced to live in overcrowded and squalid refugee camps.

In 1964, the Palestine Liberation Organization (PLO) was formed with the goal of destroying Israel and establishing a homeland for the Palestinians. Unable to mount a wide-scale military campaign against Israel, the PLO instead resorted to terrorist attacks against Israeli soldiers and citizens. Israel would always strike back at the terrorists by launching air raids at refugee camps, mostly in Jordan. Following the Six-Day War, the PLO intensified its terrorist activities, and Israel responded in kind with air strikes at Jordan.

Finally, King Hussein of Jordan decided his nation could not withstand the repeated attacks by Israel. Nor did Hussein want to risk permitting the Palestinians to draw his country and other Arab nations into a widespread conflict. He was also concerned about the stability of his own regime because many Palestinians leaders had bristled against his conservative leadership in the face of the air strikes and called for his removal. In September 1970, the king launched a war to drive the PLO out of Jordan. In the refugee camps, Hussein's war on the Palestinians came to be known as "Black September."

Some 4,000 suspected terrorists were killed by Hussein's soldiers. More than 150,000 Palestinians were driven out of refugee camps in Jordan. When PLO members resettled in refugee camps in Syria, Lebanon, and other Arab countries, they formed a new terrorist group with the aim of moving the conflict against the Israelis out of the Middle East and onto the world stage. They called themselves "Black September." They resolved to strike back at their two enemies—the Israelis, who had driven them out of the West Bank, and the Jordanians, who had forced them to flee far from their homeland.

Black September struck first in November 1971, murdering Jordanian Prime Minister Wasif Tell. Assassins gunned him down outside a hotel in Cairo, Egypt. Egyptian police quickly closed in and apprehended three terrorists responsible for the murder. As terrorist Monzer Khalifa was led away, he shouted: "We are members of Black September!"

Three weeks later, King Hussein's unfriendly regime was again targeted by Black September. Zaid el Rifai, Jordan's ambassador to Great Britain, was attacked in downtown London by a terrorist wielding a machine gun.

"I couldn't believe it," said William Parsons, a London electric-utility worker who witnessed the attack. "He leveled it at hip height, pulled the trigger, and loosed off about 30 rounds. It was like a scene from a Chicago gangster film."

Miraculously, el Rifai survived the attack—a bullet sliced through his right hand, but otherwise he was uninjured. Nevertheless, the violence directed toward the prime minister and the ambassador served Black September's purpose—to establish itself as an international terrorist organization, capable of striking quickly and ruthlessly against its enemies.

As the name suggests, terrorists attempt to terrorize, or strike fear, into a society or group of people by threatening or committing acts of violence. In the end, they hope to achieve political goals, such as changing conditions in society or even overthrowing a government.

Terrorists are frequently members of groups, although they usually act alone or in small squads. The identities of their leaders and members are often kept secret, making it difficult for law enforcement agencies to track them down or defeat the larger group. While the individual terrorist or squad may be captured or killed, the organization remains intact and authorities can only guess at its precise structure and membership. In the case of Black September, international law enforcement agencies were never sure just what type of threat the group posed, guessing its membership at between 100 and 600.

King Hussein was able to drive Black September from the country by using the army to root out all Palestinian refugees in a ruthless campaign that left many innocent people dead or homeless. In countries with democratic governments, such as the United States, an action similar to Hussein's attack would be illegal and unconstitutional.

In Jordan, the terrorists fought back against King Hussein's forces, but they were outmatched and quickly defeated. As for a direct attack on Israel, the terrorists knew that would also be futile—they could never hope to defeat the well-trained and well-armed Israeli military in a direct confrontation. For this reason, it is often said that terrorism is a tool of the weak against the strong.

Terrorists may target governments, political parties, ethnic or religious groups, corporations, or members of the news media. Sometimes they carry out political assassinations, targeting specific government leaders, such as Tell or el Rifai. But most often, the violence is directed at random victims—passengers on a bus or airplane, for example, or young people dancing in a nightclub or shopping at a mall. The randomness of the attack serves an important terrorist goal: bringing fear to, and undermining the sense of security of, large numbers of people. Simply by virtue of being in the wrong place at the wrong time, they too could be victims. Many terrorists are willing to give their own lives for the cause, acting as suicide bombers with the belief that their deeds will bring about change. Indeed, an important motive of the terrorist is to send a message. That is why terrorist groups are quick to claim responsibility for their crimes and welcome press interest in their activities.

Terrorism can happen at any time, any where; fear is its main power as a weapon of destruction. A suicide bomber targeted a bus and its occupants one Sunday morning in 1996. To go to these lengths, Palestinian Arabs apparently have a will and national identity of their own after all.

Governments have long been confounded as to the best way to deal with terrorists. A liberal government that would favor negotiating with terrorists could foster criticism that it is weak; a conservative government that refuses to negotiate and launches violent counter-strikes could be regarded as ruthless.

Terrorism is not a practice limited to the Middle East. Although, certainly, the twisted politics and fanatical beliefs of some Arabs have drawn the world's attention to such terrorist leaders as Osama bin Laden, who ordered the attacks on the World Trade Center and the Pentagon, and Omar Abdel Rahman, who led a plan to blow up the World Trade Center in New York City. Also, it is no secret that Muammar al-Qaddafi, who rules the nation of Libya, has supported and financed terrorists.

Still, terrorists have been born and raised in many free societies. Timothy McVeigh, who set the bomb that killed 168 people in the Alfred Murrah Federal Building in Oklahoma City, was considered a terrorist. In June 2001, the United States government carried out the death penalty against McVeigh.

■   ■   ■

Following the assassination of Tell and the attempt on el Rifai, leaders of Black September turned their attention to their other sworn enemy: Israel.

In May 1972, four Black September members— Ahmed Mousa Awad, Abdel Aziz el Atrash, Therese Halasseh, and Rima Tannous—boarded a Sabena Airlines flight in Brussels, Belgium, bound for Tel Aviv. Carrying guns and hand grenades, the four terrorists announced that they planned to start murdering the 91 passengers and crew members unless more than 200 Palestinian prisoners were released from Israeli jails.

The plane landed in Tel Aviv. On the ground, Israeli negotiators kept the talks with the terrorists going for 20 hours until a special unit of commandos could be summoned and prepared for a siege on the plane. Dressed as ground crew members, the commandos suddenly rushed aboard the plane and killed Awad and el Atrash. The two female terrorists, Halasseh and Tannous, were captured. One passenger was killed in the melee aboard the airliner. Later, passengers in the airliner said the Israeli commandos came aboard just as the terrorists prepared to explode a bomb.

On August 15—just 11 days before the start of the Munich Olympics—Halasseh and Tannous were sentenced by an Israeli court to life in prison.

In the refugee camps in Lebanon, Black September leaders bristled over the failure of the Sabena hijacking. They were also furious at the International Olympic Committee, which had refused their request to permit a PLO team to participate in the Munich Games. And so three Black September leaders—Abu Daoud, Fakhri al Umari and Abu Iyad—met in Rome, Italy, and hatched a plan to kidnap Israeli athletes at the Olympics and again demand the release of Palestinians held in Israeli prisons.

Luttif Afif, a 35-year-old terrorist known as "Issa," was selected to lead the mission. Afif had lived in Germany and attended school there. He knew the country and its language. Assisting Afif was another Palestinian who had spent time in Germany—Yusuf Nazzal, called "Tony." Both men were sent to Munich weeks before the Olympics began. They found jobs in the Olympic Village and soon got down to the business of planning the assault on the Israeli team. Back in the Middle East, Black September leaders drafted another six Palestinians from the refugee camps to assist Issa and Tony, and dispatched them to Munich.

When the Games got underway, the Israeli athletes and their coaches and referees took up residence in four apartments in a building on Connollystrasse—a street in the Olympic Village named for American gold medal-winner James B. Connolly. For 11 days, Issa and Tony sat in front of 31 Connollystrasse in the late summer sunshine playing chess as the world's athletes hurried by, oblivious to the plans that were being laid.

The flag of Israel flies at half-mast during a memorial service for the slain victims. The Olympic Committee's decision to continue with the games was a controversial one. In fact, some individual athletes and whole teams returned to their countries rather than compete.

Hava Tistalku! 3

Issa, Tony, and six other Palestinians arrived at the gates of the Olympic Village at about 4 A.M., September 5. They found the gates locked as well, but soon spotted some American athletes returning from a night of partying. The eight terrorists were dressed in athletic warm-up suits with their guns hidden in gym bags. They fell in behind the Americans, even traded jokes with them. When the Americans hopped over the fence, the Palestinians followed.

Six German post office workers on their way to work in the Olympic Village saw the men scaling the fence, but they had witnessed athletes climbing the fence many times in the past two weeks and, therefore, did not find the scene unusual.

"We walked for a while with the American athletes, then said goodbye," recalled Jamal Al-Gashey, one of the terrorists.

Once the Americans parted, the eight Palestinians made their way through the shadows to Connollystrasse. Just around the corner from Number 31, the eight men paused in the shadows to change out of their warm-up suits and into street clothes. They also took their automatic weapons out of their gym bags. Issa put on a white hat with the brim turned down.

By now it was 4:30 A.M., and the armed men were ready to enter Number 31. There were 24 apartments in Number 31—four occupied by the Israelis, the rest by athletes from Hong Kong and Uruguay.

They found the door to the building's foyer unlocked and entered. Jamal Al-Gashey was told to remain in the foyer and stand guard. The other seven then approached the door of Apartment One; one of the terrorists produced a key that had been obtained during the planning stages of the siege.

Inside the apartment slept Shapira as well as Kehat Shorr, coach of the rifle team; Andre Spitzer, the fencing coach; Tuvia Sokolovsky, weightlifting trainer; Jacov Springer, weightlifting referee; Yossef Gutfreund, a wrestling referee; and Weinberg.

Gutfreund had been awakened by the sounds in the foyer. He stood barefoot on the other side of the door, listening to the sounds in the foyer. And then, he opened the door—just a crack.

With just a glance, he saw the guns in the hands of the terrorists.

He slammed the door shut.

"Hava tistalku!" Gutfreund shouted in Hebrew.

In English, the words mean: "Take cover boys!"

Gutfreund threw his weight against the door. He was a big man, weighing 290 pounds.

Outside the apartment, the terrorists dropped their

keys and put their shoulders to the door. Gutfreund was able to hold them off, but not for long. With several terrorists pushing on the door, Gutfreund could hold them for just a few seconds. Finally, they burst into the room and knocked the Israeli to the floor.

Inside the bedrooms, the startled Israelis shook themselves awake. Sokolovsky darted out of his bedroom just as the Palestinians entered the apartment. He fled back into the bedroom and made his escape through the window, although he was delayed for a few seconds because he had difficulty opening the glass.

"It fell out and I jumped and began to run," he said. "The Arab terrorists started shooting at me and I could hear bullets flying near my ears."

But Sokolovsky did manage to evade the terrorists. Within seconds, he made his way out to the street and took cover in the shadows.

The other Israelis weren't so lucky. The terrorists went room to room in the apartment, rounding up the team members. When Issa burst into Weinberg's room, the former commando was ready for him. Weinberg lunged at the Black September leader with a kitchen knife; Issa was quick, darting just out of the way of the blade, although it slashed through his jacket. Issa fired his gun at Weinberg, hitting the Israeli wrestling coach in the cheek with a single shot. Another terrorist entered the room, and they dragged Weinberg out, injured and bleeding.

Black September now had six prisoners. The Palestinians tied up five of the men, but took Weinberg out of the apartment and demanded to know where the rest of the Israelis were sleeping.

They stopped first outside Apartment Two. One of the terrorists asked Weinberg whether they could find Israelis there. No, Weinberg said, the Uruguay team

An aerial view of the Munich Olympic Village where members of the Black September terrorist group abducted members of Israel's Olympic team. German police were ill-equipped and poorly prepared to deal with such a situation.

was staying in Apartment Two.

It was a lie. Five athletes from Israel were asleep inside the apartment, but the coach had somehow convinced the terrorists to move on. His lie saved the lives of the five men inside.

The terrorists moved on to Apartment Three. This time, they didn't ask Weinberg who was living in the apartment; instead, they drew out a set of keys and tried opening the locked door. Inside Apartment Three, six Israelis slept—three wrestlers and three weightlifters. Weinberg knew the personalities of most of the men inside because he had trained with them and knew them to be fighters. Months before, at a competition in Athens, Greece, Weinberg and his wrestlers found themselves in a barroom brawl with a group of Arab sailors who outnumbered the Israelis two-to-one. The wrestlers mopped the floor with the Arabs, tossing them broken and bloody into the Athens streets.

Suddenly, the lock to Apartment Three clicked open. The terrorists pushed the door open and walked into the apartment silently; Weinberg, by now bleeding profusely in the mouth, was unable to call out to his sleeping teammates.

They quickly found the bedroom where weightlifters Yossef Romano and Zeev Friedman were asleep. Staying in another bedroom in the apartment were weightlifter David Berger and wrestler Gad Tsabari, while wrestlers Mark Slavin and Eliezer Halfin occupied the third bedroom.

Tsabari was already awake, having been roused by the gunshot that struck Weinberg. He darted out of bed and opened a connecting door to find a terrorist pointing a gun at Slavin and Halfin. The terrorist quickly ordered Tsabari into the room, where he joined the other two men. Berger awoke amid the commotion, and he, too, was taken prisoner. In the other bedroom, Romano and Friedman were jostled awake and captured as well.

The Israelis were ordered out of the apartment where they joined Weinberg in the hallway. By now, Weinberg had wrapped a scarf around his face to try to stop the bleeding. The seven men were pushed down the stairs toward Apartment One.

"Let's pounce on them!" Berger hissed in Hebrew. "We have nothing to lose!"

But one of the terrorists understood Berger, and brandished his gun at the Israelis.

Just outside Apartment One, Tsabari made a bold move. He shot down a stairwell that led to a parking garage. A terrorist ran after him but Tsabari was able to make it into the garage, where he hid behind a concrete pillar.

"I felt two or three rounds being shot at me," Tsabari recalled. "I ran for my life, zigzagging to avoid the salvo of shots. I could not believe that none of them hit me. It only lasted a few minutes but every minute was as long as the years in my life."

Back upstairs, Weinberg made his move as well. Calling on his commando training, the burly coach punched one of the terrorists in the face and kicked the gun out of the hands of another.

Alas, there were too many armed men for even a trained Israeli commando to overcome. One of the terrorists leveled his machine gun at Weinberg and shot him in the chest.

He was the first to die.

■   ■   ■

In 1950, the Knesset—the legislature of Israel—adopted a law known as "The Law of Return." The law recognized the right of all Jews to emigrate to Israel and become Israeli citizens.

Over the centuries, Jews had found themselves living far from their homeland established hundreds of years before the birth of Christ by the Israelite kings Saul, David, and Solomon. The scattering of Jews throughout the world was known as the "diaspora," a Greek word meaning "dispersion."

Weightlifter David Marc Berger, 28, was born and raised in the Cleveland, Ohio, suburb of Shaker Heights. He was the son of a doctor. He was an American, but under the Law of Return he was eligible to become a member of the Israeli Olympic team.

In America, Berger attended Tulane University in Louisiana and Columbia University in New York, where he obtained a degree in law. He planned to put his career as an attorney on hold, though, while

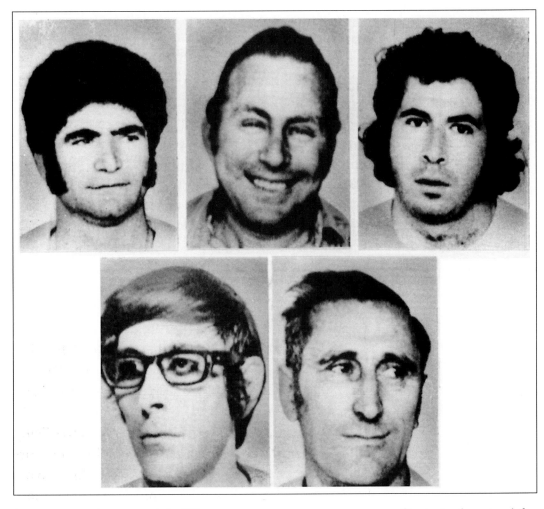

he competed as a weightlifter.

Under American law, Berger held dual nationality—meaning he was a citizen of both the United States and Israel. The United States government permits its citizens to hold dual nationality as long as they don't renounce their American citizenship.

Berger first arrived in Israel in 1969 as a member of the U.S. team for the Macabee Games, where he won a gold medal as a middleweight. A year later, Berger returned to Israel and, invoking the Law of Return, became a member of the Israeli weightlifting team and began competing as an

Clockwise from top left: Yossef Romano, Amitzor Shapira, David Berger, (bottom right) Kehat Shorr, Andre Spitzer (bottom right)

Israeli in international competitions. Berger had decided to stay in Israel following the Olympics. He had been studying Hebrew and after his return from Munich, Berger intended to fulfill his military obligation by joining the Israel Defense Force. He also planned to marry and eventually practice law in Israel.

Mark Slavin, 18, was Moshe Weinberg's favorite wrestler. His coach called him "Little Mark." Slavin had emigrated from the Soviet Union just a few months before the Olympics and lived on a communal farm known as a "kibbutz." In the Soviet Union, Slavin had been openly defiant of the communist government where he demonstrated for the rights of the "refuseniks," Jewish people in the Soviet Union who had been denied the right to emigrate to Israel.

Wrestler Eliezer Halfin, 24, had also emigrated from the Soviet Union, arriving in 1968. In Tel Aviv, he worked as a garage mechanic. He was unmarried.

Weightlifter Zeev Friedman, 28, arrived in Israel in 1960 from Poland. He worked as a physical education teacher in a suburb of the Israeli city of Haifa. Friedman was also unmarried.

Weightlifter Yossef Romano, 32, was born in the North African nation of Libya. Back home in Israel, Romano worked as a window decorator, and had a wife and three daughters. Romano was forced to drop out of the competition in Munich because he injured a leg during a lift. For the remainder of the Olympics, Romano hobbled around the village on crutches. He planned to have an operation on his injured leg when he returned in Israel.

Amitzur Shapira, 40, was the team's track-and-field coach. He taught physical education in Israel, where he had a wife and four children. On the day the terrorists broke into 31 Connollystrasse, Shapira was to accompany Esther Shahamorov to the semifinals in her competition.

Kehat Shorr, 53, was the coach of the rifle team. In Israel, Shorr served in the Defense Ministry, the civilian agency that oversees the military. He was married and had a daughter. Shorr had emigrated to Israel from Romania.

Andre Spitzer, 27, was the fencing team coach. He had also come to Israel from Romania, arriving in 1964. He had a wife and two-month-old daughter.

Jacov Springer, 52, was a weightlifting referee. An immigrant from Poland, Springer taught physical education at a school near Tel Aviv.

Yossef Gutfreund, 40, was a wrestling referee. He was married, and had two daughters. In Israel, Gutfreund was a merchant in the Israeli capital of Jerusalem.

■　■　■

Jerusalem is not only the Israeli capital, it is one of Judaism's holiest cities. In biblical times it served as the home of Kings David and Solomon, who built many palaces and other ornate buildings in the city. Solomon built a great house of worship in the city, known today as the Temple Mount. In the Jewish religion, places of worship are called temples or synagogues.

Solomon also surrounded the city with a wall. Later, King Herod erected a great temple, its Western Wall remains standing today. Jews throughout the world make pilgrimages to the Western Wall, which they regard as one of their religion's most sacred sites.

Christians regard Jerusalem as a holy city as well. Jesus Christ spent his last days on Earth in Jerusalem. During the era of the Roman Empire, the Church of the Holy Sepulcher was built by Emperor Constantine. Other rulers of Rome also erected Christian churches and, indeed, for centuries after the death of Christ the city was dominated by Christians.

The holy city of Jerusalem is a microcosm of the larger Arab-Israeli conflict. Here, Jewish, Muslim, and Christian cultures exist practically on top of each other, leading to inevitable clashes. This Muslim church, the Dome of the Rock, was built in the seventh century right above an earlier Jewish holy site, the altar of the Temple Mount.

In the seventh century Muslims swept into the city, drove out the Christians and established their own mosques and shrines where they could worship their god, Allah. It was during this period that the Mosque of Umar was erected in Jerusalem. Known as the "Dome of the Rock," the mosque is built on the site where Muhammad is said to have ascended to heaven. A prophet and teacher, Muhammad is the founder of the Islamic faith—the religion practiced by millions of people.

But the Dome of the Rock symbolizes more than just the birthplace of Islam. It is also a symbol of the conflict that exists between Jews and Muslims, because the Dome of the Rock is built over the altar of the Temple Mount. Since the Six-Day War in 1967, the entire city of Jerusalem, including the Dome of the Rock, has been under the control of the Israelis.

Over the centuries, Jews, Christians, and Muslims have been forced to live in Jerusalem as unfriendly neighbors, always watching one another's moves, ever on the lookout for trouble.

■   ■   ■

The eight Palestinians holding the Israelis captive did not regard themselves as terrorists. In the Arabic language, they called themselves "fedayeen"—fighters for freedom.

Not all the fedayeen in Munich were Muslims. Issa was the son of a Christian father and, ironically, a Jewish mother. And yet, he was totally devoted to the Palestinian cause, which included destruction of Israel. Issa was born in Nazareth—the town holy to Christians as a place where Jesus lived; now, it is part of Israel.

Unlike the others, though, Issa had not lived in a refugee camp. Indeed, his father was a successful businessman who could afford to send Issa to expensive schools. In 1958, Issa traveled to Germany to study civil engineering; later he found a job in France. But he was drawn to the Palestinian movement, and in 1966 joined Al Fatah—the armed unit of the Palestine Liberation Organization. In September 1970, he fought against King Hussein's troops in Jordan. Following the war against Jordan, Issa returned to Germany where he married. Issa had three brothers—all were in Black September, and two were in Israeli jails.

The other fedayeen had spent their childhoods in the overcrowded refugee camps of the Middle East. For the refugees, food was provided by the United Nations Relief and Works Agency, but families often went hungry. In the camps, refugees lived in tents or huts they built out of scraps of wood and tin. Disease was rampant, water often scarce. The children wore rags, their shoes were made from old rubber tires.

Jamal Al-Gashey recalled his years growing up in one of the camps.

"I was raised on my family's stories about Palestine, the paradise we were driven from, about how the Jews had stolen our land and expelled us from it, how the Arab leaders had betrayed us," he said. "When I was growing up, I thought that there was no future for us unless we returned to Palestine, and that if we didn't return, I would spend my whole life as a refugee, deprived of any kind of human rights."

■   ■   ■

With the racket created by the shots fired at Tsabari as well as in the murder of Weinberg, the terrorists decided to abandon their plans to round up the remaining members of the Israeli team. Outside, lights started flickering on in apartments along Connollystrasse. Surely, people had heard the shots and the police would be arriving soon to investigate. The Palestinians now had 10 team members captive—five in the hallway and five held in Apartment One. The terrorists ordered the five men in the hallway to proceed to Apartment One.

One of the terrorists shoved Romano toward the apartment. The burly weightlifter instead turned, threw down his crutches and lunged at the terrorist. He managed to grab the man's gun, but another terrorist fired off a burst and killed Romano.

"It was necessary and beyond anyone's control," said Jamal Al-Gashey. "They nearly caused the failure of the operation. They were strong athletes." Romano, Al-Gashey said, "was another powerful athlete who attacked a member of our group and grabbed his gun,

and had almost wrestled it from his hand, so we had to open fire on him as well."

The four surviving men in the hallway were herded into the apartment, where they joined their teammates in one of the bedrooms. All nine men were tied up.

The first policeman arrived at Connollystrasse at 4:50 A.M. A German cleaning woman on her way to work heard the shots and called the security office in the Olympic Village. The officer, armed with only a walkie-talkie, approached the apartment building slowly. Suddenly, the door to the building opened and the policeman saw a terrorist wearing a ski mask and brandishing a machine gun.

After a few seconds, the door closed.

Suspected Arab terrorists are often pursued even outside Israel by Israeli commandos. Masked Palestinian terrorists march during a rally at Gaza University in support of a comrade killed in Tunisia by Israeli Special Forces.

The End of Innocence

German police dressed in sweat suits to disguise themselves as athletes and climbed onto a roof near No. 31 Connollystrasse in the Olympic Village. American camera crews also caught their movements on a live television broadcast that could possibly also be viewed by the terrorists. Officials recalled the police rather than risk their lives.

4

Before cable television made ESPN and other 24-hour sports networks possible, Americans received their televised sports in small doses. Indeed, back in the 1950s and 1960s, most sports on TV were telecast on the weekends, and hardly ever in the evening "prime time" hours, when most people were at home watching their television screens. Even such big events as the World Series and Super Bowl were played in the afternoons.

One very popular show on TV during the 1960s and 1970s was "Wide World of Sports," broadcast on the ABC television network. The program, which occasionally still airs today, gave Americans a view of the type of sports they didn't have a chance to see in person— skiing in Austria, surfing in Hawaii, and cliff diving in Acapulco,

Mexico, were some of the events covered by the program's globe-trotting correspondents.

Hosting the program was veteran TV sportscaster Jim McKay. Each week, he opened the show with the promise that viewers would share in the "thrill of victory" and the "agony of defeat."

When ABC won the right to broadcast the 1972 Munich Olympics, McKay was selected to anchor the coverage from a TV studio erected in the heart of the Olympic Village. And ABC made the innovative decision that the Olympics would be telecast live and in prime time. Advances in technology made it possible for the network to bounce its transmissions off satellites flying in space so that American viewers could see live coverage of events occurring thousands of miles away. Each evening during the Olympics, millions of Americans tuned in to the network's coverage.

On the morning of September 5, McKay was awakened in his Munich hotel room by a ringing telephone. It was an ABC executive calling, reporting to McKay that terrorists had killed a member of the Israeli team and taken others hostage. He was told to hurry to the studio in the Olympic Village because the network planned to televise coverage of the siege to its American audience. McKay glanced at the clock: 8 A.M. On the East Coast in America it was 2 A.M.

McKay threw on his clothes and rushed to the television studio in the Olympic Village, just 300 feet from 31 Connollystrasse. He arrived to find the building housing the studio ringed with Munich police officers—this time they were heavily armed. The German authorities believed the television studio, with its capacity to broadcast a message to a worldwide audience—would be a likely target for a terrorist siege.

Once arriving in the studio, McKay learned that the network was able to train a single camera onto the building where the hostages were held. Also, a young network correspondent, Peter Jennings, found his way into an apartment building closer to the scene of the crisis. Jennings had made it into an apartment occupied by Italian Olympic athletes, just 150 feet from 31 Connollystrasse. He had a clear view of the scene, and would be reporting in by telephone throughout the day. John Wilcox, an associate producer for ABC, disguised himself as an athlete and managed to slip past police into a building just across the street from 31 Connollystrasse. He had no telephone, but could communicate with the network through a walkie-talkie.

"In all my days in television, some 18,000 all told, one day stands out as the most significant of all: September 5, 1972," McKay said. "It marked the halfway point of my career and the end of innocence for sport."

In a few short hours, Americans would rise from their beds and gulp down their morning cups of coffee. And when they turned on their TVs to catch a glimpse of the news before heading off to work, they would be greeted by the image of a terrorist in a ski mask, machine gun slung over his shoulder, standing guard on the balcony of Apartment One in Number 31 Connollystrasse.

■　　■　　■

Manfred Schreiber was also awakened by a phone call reporting details of the siege. His call came at 5 A.M., just 10 minutes after the Munich policeman had come face to face with the terrorist. Schreiber was the 46-year-old police chief of Munich. He immediately ordered dozens of Munich police officers to the scene

Peter Jennings, an ABC news correspondent on site in Munich, had a direct view of activities outside the Israelis' building. Jennings' colleague and ABC sports anchor, Jim McKay, called the events of September 5 ". . . the end of innocence for sport."

with instructions to surround the building. He also made a call himself, dialing Bruno Merck, a Bavarian ministry official who oversaw the Munich police. Merck would, in turn, make contact with higher-ranking German officials, who would bring word of the crisis to Willie Brandt, the chancellor of Germany. The Israeli government was also contacted—Israeli Prime Minister Golda Meir was awakened and told the news.

It was now 5:10 A.M. Back on Connollystrasse, a Munich police officer approached Number 31. His arms were raised, showing he carried no weapon. The policeman stopped in front of the building as a window opened on the second floor. Two pieces of paper were tossed out the window, floating down to the street at the feet of the police officer. The papers contained Black September's demands: the release of 234 Palestinians held in Israeli jails as well as two terrorists held in German prisons— Andreas Baader and Ulrike Meinhof, leaders of a German gang that had helped Black September plan and execute some of its missions.

Suddenly, the blood-soaked body of Moshe Weinberg was tossed out the window. It hurtled to the ground and struck the concrete with a thud. A few minutes later, the terrorists permitted an ambulance crew to approach the building and retrieve Weinberg's body. At this time, the body of Yossef Romano was still inside Number 31; authorities did not know a second hostage had been murdered.

The terrorists set a deadline of 9 A.M. for the release of the prisoners. If Israel and Germany refused their demands, the terrorists intended to begin executing their prisoners.

Schreiber hurried to the Olympic Village where he took command of the police response. He resolved to open a channel of communications with the terrorists and find out if there was a way to negotiate an end to the crisis.

Annaliese Graes, a 42-year-old policewoman, was assigned to open that channel of communications. Schreiber wanted a woman to talk to the terrorists because he felt they would be less intimidated by a female. At 8:10 A.M.—less than an hour from the deadline—Graes walked slowly down Connollystrasse,

Dr. Manfred Schreiber, Munich's Chief of Police, looks at his watch while attempting to negotiate with one of the Palestinian terrorists. To their frustration, there was little German officials could do other than convey Black September's demands to the Israeli government.

stopping just a few feet from the door of Number 31.

After a few seconds, Issa appeared at the door. He was wearing the white hat he had donned in the shadows of Connollystrasse moments before the siege.

"What kind of rubbish is this?" Graes asked.

"This has nothing to do with you or Germany," said Issa.

"We can do nothing about freeing all those political prisoners you want from Israel," Graes said. "We can only transmit your terms. Why not give us conditions that are possible for us to meet?"

"Free all prisoners," Issa said, "or the hostages will die."

■   ■   ■

Incredibly, as the Munich police and Black September terrorists settled in for a standoff, the Games continued. Just 400 yards from Connollystrasse, 2,000 fans gathered to watch a volleyball match between the German and Japanese teams. American boxer Duane Bobick, a heavy favorite to win a gold medal, prepared for a bout that morning. Elsewhere, athletes made their way to Olympic Stadium, where competitions in track and field were beginning to heat up.

Not all was routine. Mark Spitz, fresh from his triumphs in the swimming competitions, left Munich that morning. Although his competitions were over, Spitz had intended to remain in the Olympic Village until the closing ceremonies, which were often a moving and emotional experience for the participants as well as an opportunity for the world's athletes to share one final moment of fellowship before they departed for their home countries.

But Spitz was a Jew, and American authorities feared there could be more Palestinian terrorists lurking in the Olympic Village and his life could be in danger. Spitz had, in fact, been a participant in the Macabee Games and had become friendly with many of the Israeli athletes, including Moshe Weinberg. When reporters tracked him down at the Munich airport that morning, he brushed by them with a terse "No comment" as he boarded his plane.

■   ■   ■

Annaliese asked Issa for more time. She told the terrorist that German authorities had just made contact with Israeli officials, and that leaders in Jerusalem had not yet made a decision on Black September's demands. Issa agreed to an extension. Israel now had until noon.

German Chancellor Willie Brandt had, in fact, already been in contact with Israeli Prime Minister Golda Meir.

"I want to assure you that I will do everything possible to free the Israeli athletes," Brandt said. "I am worried about these fedayeen in the Village. Without trying to influence your decisions, I must say that, in your place, I would make some gesture, if only the slightest, to calm them down."

Brandt was asking for the impossible. Israeli leaders had long ago made it their government's official policy not to negotiate with terrorists. Indeed, they considered hostages prisoners of war. Just months before, when the Black September terrorists hijacked the Belgium plane, Israel had opened negotiations with the Palestinians aboard, but just so that its commandos had time to plan and execute a rescue mission. Then, as now, Israel had no intentions to meet the demands of the terrorists.

"My position," Meir told Brandt, "is that under no conditions will Israel make the slightest concession to terrorist blackmail. My government is unanimously behind me on this."

Still, Brandt pressed the prime minister. He told her that Germany intended to release Andreas Baader and Ulrike Meinhof. "That is all I have the power to do," Brandt said.

■   ■   ■

Just after 9 A.M. Tony appeared at the window of Number 31 and motioned for Annaliese to approach the building. Tony tossed a sheet of paper down to the

policewoman. It was a new set of demands. It read:

"The arrogant attitude of Israel's militaristic authorities and their refusal to comply with our demands have not caused us to forget our humane feelings, and we will continue to try to find a way to spare the Israeli prisoners, on the following terms:

"The German Federal Republic (GFR) must announce that it agrees to have the Israeli prisoners transferred to any other location designated by our revolutionary forces in Olympic Village.

"The GFR must put at the disposal of our forces three airplanes on which the Israeli prisoners and our

One of the terrorists appeared on the balcony wearing a ski mask to throw out Black September's requirements for the hostages' survival: 234 Palestinians held in Israeli jails and two in German jails had to be released. "Free all prisoners or the hostages will die."

Golda Meir, Israeli Prime Minister, refused to submit to the terrorists demands. Officials would only warn the hostages' families of the dangerous situation unfolding in Munich. The two Palestinians in German jails were quickly released, however.

armed forces will fly, in three successive departures, toward a destination chosen by us. Each plane will leave Munich about one hour after the previous one arrives at its destination.

"Any attempt to sabotage our operation will result in immediate liquidation of all Israeli prisoners, for which the GFR will bear total responsibility.

"The ultimatum expires three hours from now; that is, at noon. The GFR will be responsible for the results of this decision.

"At the expiration of this ultimatum, if our demand to leave German territory has not been complied with, our revolutionary forces are instructed to use just and revolutionary force to give a severe lesson to the warmongering heads of the Israeli military machine and the GFR for its arrogance.

"Revolutionaries of the world, unite."

The message was signed "IBSO"—the International Black September Organization.

■   ■   ■

As the hours dragged on, McKay stayed at his post in the TV studio, reporting the events as they unfolded to his audience in America. Truthfully, though, there wasn't much in the way of information leaking out of police headquarters. The camera trained on Number 31 could simply observe the scene, while the network's two correspondents hidden at their posts close to the action could only guess at what could be happening.

Indeed, the German police had not even publicly identified the group holding the Israelis as Black September. But Jennings, who had covered international news for ABC, was aware of the unrest in the Middle East and he surmised that the siege could be a Black September mission.

McKay said: "All we saw on the screen was the front of a building, the lookouts, an occasional negotiator going in. There were no reports of an agreement. The picture was unchanging, yet the feeling of tension was growing, not only on the scene, but, as we learned later, all across America. People stopped their working day to watch—in homes and offices, through appliance-store windows."

The television coverage may have been riveting to Americans as well as viewers in other countries tuned into the coverage, but it was frustrating to the Munich police. ABC's camera caught German sharpshooters edging their way along rooftops toward Number 31 Connollystrasse. Sound engineers at the studio had even found a way to intercept German police radio messages, so the audience at home heard the actual coded messages from police headquarters to the men on the rooftops. "Samira to Eagle, the sky is clear," one transmission said.

Peter Jennings, hidden on a balcony just 150 feet from Number 31, recalled: "I remember when the Germans looked like they were going to bring a commando team in and try to get into 31 from the top. I remember feeling very strongly that this might end badly."

When the German police realized that the terrorists were likely watching TV coverage of the siege in Apartment One, and were aware of the positions of the sharpshooters, they called them back.

■   ■   ■

In Israel, officials had the somber duty of finding the relatives of the hostages and telling them of the danger. In Miriam Weinberg's case, they would have to tell her that her husband was already dead.

Not all the families were in Israel. During the Olympics, Ankie Spitzer, the wife of fencing coach Andre Spitzer, was staying at her parents' home in the Netherlands. At 9:30 A.M. on the morning of September 5, police in Munich reached her by telephone to report that her husband was a captive of terrorists.

Before he left for the Munich Games, Andre told his wife: "The idea of the Olympics is the fact that you can forget that you're two nations, or two warring nations, and you can come together in sport, and through sport find the good in each other and make friendships, forge relationships, and find brotherhood with each other. That appeals to me greatly."

Ankie had at first planned to accompany Andre to Munich, but shortly before the Games started their daughter, Anouk, became ill. Ankie's brother was a pediatrician in the Netherlands, and Ankie decided to take the baby to her brother for treatment. Still, the Netherlands is just west of Germany, and while Anouk was under her uncle's care Ankie managed to make a quick dash to Munich.

She found Andre living up to the pledge of peace he expressed to her some weeks before. During the fencing competition, Andre approached members of the Lebanese team to compare results. Lebanon, situated on Israel's northern border, is a nation often hostile to Israel. Indeed, it is the location of many Palestinian refugee camps.

But Andre managed to bond with the Lebanese athletes. They spent several minutes talking about their competitions, then shook hands as they parted company. When Andre joined Ankie later, he was flushed with pride at having been able to break through the tensions that separated the Israeli and Lebanese people.

"This is what I was dreaming about," he told Ankie. "I knew it was going to happen."

Later, the couple left Munich for a few days to check in on Anouk. Once they were assured by Ankie's brother that their daughter was fine, Andre returned to Munich. Ankie chose to stay with the baby.

■   ■   ■

During the negotiations Manfred Schreiber approached Number 31 to speak directly with Issa.

"It occurred to me," the police chief said later, "that I might try to take him hostage. He must have sensed what I was thinking. 'Do you want to take me?' he asked, opening his hand. I saw a hand grenade. He had his thumb on the pin."

Hans-Dietrich Genscher, West Germany Interior Minister, continues negotiating with Black September members. The terrorists decided to demand passage to Egypt for themselves and the hostages. Egypt, they felt, would be more successful at working with Israel to release the Palestinian prisoners.

West German Interior Minister Hans-Dietrich Genscher was now in charge of the negotiations. Genscher told Issa the Germans would pay money to the terrorists if they released the hostages. Issa turned him down. Next, Genscher offered himself and other German officials as hostages to take the place of the Israelis.

"You know what happened to Jews in the Third Reich," he told Issa, "and you have to understand that this cannot happen in Germany. For this reason I beg you to do this exchange."

But again, Issa refused.

Genscher suspected that the hostages may already be dead. He asked to be taken into Apartment One so that he could speak with the Israelis. With the 3 P.M. deadline approaching, he also asked for more time.

The Palestinians granted Genscher permission to enter Apartment One for a short visit. He was led into the bedroom where he saw the nine athletes, their hands and feet tied, sitting on a bed.

"I talked to one," Genscher reported after leaving the apartment. "I asked him how he felt. He said all right. He hoped we were doing something."

Genscher convinced Issa that Israel had given in to the demands, and that the Palestinians would be freed from the prisons but that it would take several hours. At that point, Issa agreed to another extension. Genscher left the apartment, relieved that he had bought more time.

West German police run
for position at Munich's
Olympic Village. A nearby
military airbase, Fürstenfeldbruck, was designated
as the departure point for
the hostages and terrorists
to leave for Egypt.

Fürstenfeldbruck 5

B ut Israel had not given in to the demands of the terrorists. Golda
Meir and members of her cabinet had resolved not to be black-
mailed by the Palestinians. There had been some discussion in
Jerusalem about dispatching a team of commandos to Munich for a rescue
mission. In fact, a team of commandos was assembled under the leadership
of a young Army commander named Ehud Barak. The team began
preparing for an assault and awaited orders to depart for Germany.

The Germans resisted the idea of Israel launching a commando raid on 31
Connollystrasse. Willie Brandt decided it was Germany's responsibility to assure
the safety of the Olympic athletes. And so, he told Meir that if it came down to
staging a rescue mission, the German police would plan and execute the effort.

The truth was, though, that the Germans were ill-prepared to deal with
terrorists. The Munich police had no training in antiterrorist operations and,

unlike the Israeli commandos, they were hardly battle-trained fighters.

And Brandt and Genscher still maintained hope that the crisis could be defused through negotiations, and that further bloodshed could be avoided.

But the clock was ticking toward the new Palestinian deadline, now set for 5 P.M. Evening had started to fall on Munich. The International Olympic Committee had finally called a halt to the competitions until the crisis had ended. Athletes who were permitted to return to their apartments in the Olympic Village—well away from the scene of the siege—waited nervously for news.

Genscher, accompanied by other German officials, approached Issa again. They told the terrorist leader that Israel had asked for more time to release the prisoners. Issa accused the Germans of lying. Genscher and the others tried very hard to keep their tempers. "Germany is doing all it can!" Genscher pleaded.

Issa told the Germans he had grown frustrated with their efforts to solve the crisis, so he proposed a new idea: Would Germany agree to supply a plane to fly all hostages and fedayeen to Cairo, Egypt? Issa said he believed the Egyptians, who by the 1970s had become a moderating force in Middle East politics, would be better able to deal with the hard-line Israelis.

The Germans weren't happy with the idea, but since Issa had agreed to extend the deadline again—this time until 7 P.M. if they agreed to the plan—they assured the terrorist they would propose it to their government.

Brandt resisted Issa's proposal. The German chancellor decided that no plane carrying Israeli hostages would depart from Germany. "That would be impossible for an honorable country to allow happen," Brandt said. "We are responsible for the fate of these people."

By now, it was clear to the Germans that they would

have to launch a rescue mission. In fact, hours before, Schreiber, the police chief, had started recruiting volunteers from the ranks of the Munich police. When Genscher emerged from Apartment One after speaking with the hostages, Schreiber and other police officials debriefed the minister about the layout of the apartment, the positions of the armed men, and the conditions of the hostages. After speaking with Genscher, the police had concluded that 31 Connollystrasse was being defended like a fortress, and it would be impossible to storm the building without risking the lives of the hostages.

And so it was decided that the rescue mission would have to be launched outside the building—either en route to the airport or actually at the airport before the terrorists and hostages boarded the plane.

Just before 7 P.M., Genscher approached Issa and told him Black September's demands for transit to Egypt would be granted. According to the plan, a bus would take them to the main plaza inside the Olympic Village, where two helicopters would be waiting to fly them to Fürstenfeldbruck, a German military air base 16 miles away. At the airport, the Palestinians and Israelis would board a plane for Egypt. Again, Genscher asked for more time. Genscher could tell Issa was suspicious, but the Black September leader agreed to another extension of the deadline—this time to 10 P.M.

As Genscher left the building's entrance, Issa called Annaliese Graes over.

"I bet you 20 deutschmarks there will be an attack on us and I will lose my life," he told her.

■　　■　　■

The Germans realized now they were out of time and out of options. They devised a plan to attack the terrorists at

Fürstenfeldbruck. Sharpshooters were to be hidden at the airfield, surrounding the helicopter pad. When the two helicopters landed, they were to shoot the terrorists. Issa was to be the primary target; it was hoped that if the leader was first to die, the other terrorists would surrender. If not, the Germans were prepared to shoot all the Palestinians.

Issa suspected an ambush and made plans to stave off an attack at the airfield. He told the other terrorists to be on their guard at Fürstenfeldbruck. When they transferred the hostages from the helicopters to the plane, they planned to move them across the open airfield in small groups. That way, if one group was attacked, the terrorists would still be in control of other hostages.

Just before 10 P.M., a large, dark green bus entered the basement parking garage below 31 Connollystrasse—the same garage where, some 17 hours before Gad Tsabari had escaped by dodging bullets and zigzagging around concrete pillars. The driver was a volunteer. He parked close to the entrance that led upstairs.

At 10:03 P.M., the hostages were pushed out the door of Apartment One and led down the stairs to the parking garage. Each hostage had been blindfolded. The nervous terrorists flashed their guns, kept themselves covered and led the hostages aboard the bus. The vehicle rolled away; a camera recorded a grainy black-and-white image of the bus disappearing into the shadows of the Munich night.

Minutes later, the Munich police burst into Apartment One, where they found the body of Yossef Romano.

Outside the fence of the Olympic Village, thousands of people had gathered, hoping to catch a glimpse of the terrorists. The crowds were kept back from the plaza by the Munich police, yet they were close enough to see the bus arrive. Electricity shot through the crowd. Hundreds of flash bulbs went off. Issa ignored the spectators and inspected the helicopters. He suspected a trap.

The hostages were transferred and the helicopters lifted off. Just a few feet away from the plaza, Jim McKay sat in the Olympic Village television studio, facing the camera. He had been broadcasting the unfolding drama nonstop since arriving in the studio that morning. Now, McKay could feel the choppers leave the ground.

"The helicopters take off, their little red identification lights blinking in the darkness," McKay said. "In the studio, we can feel the vibration as they clatter out of the village, only 50 feet or so over the heads of the crowd at the fence. Several thousand people are gathered in the crowd, staring up at the helicopters helplessly. Our daughter, Mary, is there, and later says to me, 'Dad, they were so close that you felt you could almost touch them. Yet, no one could do anything to help them.'"

An Army bus carried hostages from underneath No. 31 Connollystrasse to a nearby helicopter pad for the next leg of their short journey to Fürstenfeldbruck.

■   ■   ■

Parked at Fürstenfeldbruck was a Boeing 727 airliner borrowed from Lufthansa, the German national airline. Its jet engines were idling. According to the plan, the helicopters were to land in front of the Fürstenfeldbruck control tower, an area bathed in spotlights.

Before leaving the Olympic Village, Issa told the Germans he intended to leave the hostages behind in the helicopters and, along with another terrorist, take a few minutes to inspect the 727. The Germans had decided to shoot Issa and the other terrorist as they returned to the helicopters after inspecting the plane. The other terrorists would then be picked off at the helicopters if they did not surrender.

The plan had a serious flaw. Throughout the day, the Germans believed there were five terrorists in Apartment One. Only when they left the apartment to board the bus did the police learn there were eight armed men. But they had dispatched just five sharpshooters to Fürstenfeldbruck. It meant that there were more terrorists than sharpshooters. Incredibly, when the Munich police discovered this fact, they never thought of calling Fürstenfeldbruck to warn the sharpshooters of the glitch.

Three of the sharpshooters were stationed on the roof of a small office building that overlooked the landing site. One sharpshooter was hidden behind a low garden wall, directly behind the landing site. The final sharpshooter hid behind a truck parked next to the Lufthansa plane.

Dozens of other armed police officers were stationed around the airfield as well.

Another plan by the Germans went awry as well. Munich police officers were supposed to have been stationed on the airliner disguised as flight crew members. But when the police officers entered the narrow 727 cabin, they decided that the plane would offer little protection if they found themselves in a gun battle with the terrorists. So with the helicopters just a few minutes from arrival at Fürstenfeldbruck, the police aboard the plane abandoned their positions.

"It was nothing more than a suicide mission that was cancelled unanimously," said Munich police detective Heinz Hohensinn, who had been aboard the plane.

The helicopters arrived just after 10:30 P.M. The two choppers circled the field, then landed.

Issa, Tony, and two other terrorists stepped off one helicopter, their guns raised. Above them, on the roof of the office building, three German sharpshooters trained their sights on the Palestinians.

The helicopters had landed about 500 feet from the plane. Issa and Tony approached the plane slowly and went on board to conduct their inspection. When Issa found no flight crew on board, he knew it was a trap— the Germans had never intended to permit the plane to take off.

Issa and Tony quickly left the plane, shouting as they ran back toward the helicopters. Three Palestinians were standing outside the helicopters; the others were still inside the choppers.

Issa and Tony were now halfway back to the helicopters. Clearly, the snipers on the rooftop could see the three armed men standing by the choppers suspected something was wrong; they had raised their guns.

The order was given. Shots burst from the roof. One terrorist standing by the helicopter was killed, the other two dived away from the shots, seeking safety under the helicopter.

The four Germans who had served as the flight crews aboard the choppers dashed for cover. Tony and Issa approached the helicopters. Tony was hit in the leg and collapsed, but Issa was able to dive for cover.

A firefight ensued; thousands of bullets raked the airfield. The terrorists managed to shoot out the searchlights throwing the field into darkness, but bright shots exploding from gun barrels constantly pierced the night.

Hundreds of witnesses saw the helicopter with hostages take off yet all were powerless to help in such a crowded location. "I bet you 20 deutschmarks there will be an attack on us and I will lose my life," one of the terrorists predicted to a German policewoman.

Issa had survived the initial volley and was now hidden under a helicopter, sweeping the field with machine gun fire.

The Germans did score some hits. Jamal Al-Gashey was hit in the hand. Another terrorist was hit in the chest. After about an hour of the two sides firing wild shots at each other, the pace of the battle slowed. Now, the police and terrorists seemed content to throw an occasional shot across the airfield.

■   ■   ■

Back at the TV studio, mixed reports were arriving from Fürstenfeldbruck. McKay did what he could to report the news to America, but throughout the evening he was forced to tell viewers that all reports were unconfirmed, and journalists had been unable to get close enough to the airfield to learn the truth.

"There is no substantive word of what is happening at the airport—except for one brief frightening report: 'All hell is breaking loose out here!'" McKay told his audience.

As the shootout erupted McKay received information from a German official stating that the hostages had been freed.

Just past 11 P.M., he was handed this news release: "An officer of the Munich police states that all hostages have been freed and four of the terrorists captured. From authoritative sources at the air base at Fürstenfeldbruck, it is learned that one Palestinian has gotten away and several persons have been injured, among them perhaps some of the hostages."

■   ■   ■

Just after midnight, four armored assault vehicles arrived at Fürstenfeldbruck. They took positions around the helicopters, aiming to move in on the terrorists. Clearly, the Palestinians were menaced by the armored vehicles, which would be able to withstand Black September's machine gun fire.

The ordeal of the Israeli hostages was about to end in tragedy.

Inside one of the helicopters, a terrorist shot Springer, Halfin, Friedman, and Berger. The man then leaped out of the chopper, pulled the pin of his hand grenade, and tossed it back in. The aircraft exploded into a fireball.

Issa jumped out from beneath the other helicopter and started strafing the field with his machine gun. He was killed by one of the rooftop sharpshooters. Also killed in the exchange of gunfire was the terrorist who tossed the hand grenade.

Five Israelis were in the other helicopter. A terrorist climbed aboard and shot them. Gutfreund, Shorr, Slavin, Spitzer, and Shapira were all murdered.

The battle was still not over.

Terrorist Khalid Jawad dashed across the tarmac, attempting to escape. He was cut down by the sharpshooter stationed behind the garden wall. Seven shots sliced through his body.

Jawad collapsed near the place on the airfield where Ganner Ebel, one of the German helicopter pilots, had taken cover. The dash of the Palestinian had drawn fire from one of the armored cars. Ebel was wounded by a stray bullet fired from the armored car. So was the sharpshooter who killed Jawad.

By now, the fire crews at Fürstenfeldbruck had arrived at the scene and attempted to put out the blaze engulfing the burning helicopter. But there were still four armed terrorists hiding under the other helicopter, and they drove off the fire crews with their machine guns.

Minutes later, a sharpshooter killed another terrorist. It was now 12:30 A.M., the morning of September 6.

The shooting had stopped. Slowly, the police approached the two helicopters. They found two of the surviving terrorists hiding amid the wreckage of the burned out helicopter; the third survivor was found hiding among the bodies of the dead.

The three captured men were Jamal Al-Gashey, Adnan Al-Gashey, and Mohammed Safady. Jamal Al-Gashey had been shot in the hand; the others were uninjured. They were taken to a Munich jail. There was one more casualty—at some point during the battle, a German policeman had been killed in the crossfire.

Just before 5 A.M.—some 25 hours after Issa and the other Palestinians hopped over the fence of the Olympic Village, German police at Fürstenfeldbruck

issued a news release. The information was relayed to Jim McKay at the Olympic Village television studio. It was now shortly before 11 P.M. on the East Coast of the United States.

McKay stared at the camera, his face displaying the weight of the horror he was about to deliver.

He said: "When I was a boy, my father told me that in life, our greatest ambitions and worst fears are seldom realized. Tonight, our worst fears have been realized. Two of the hostages were killed in their rooms this morning—excuse me, that's yesterday morning. Nine others were killed at the airport tonight."

McKay paused for what seemed like an eternity.

And then, he said: "They're all gone."

Mistaken information, and poor communications and tactics led to the failure of the siege by German officials at Fürstenfeldbruck. Realizing the hopelessness of their situation, the terrorists set fire to the helicopters to provide cover from snipers and shot the remaining hostages before they were killed themselves.

Wrath of God

Flowers lay at the base of the Olympic torch for the memorial service after the shootout at Fürstenfeldbruck. The 80,000 seat stadium filled with spectators paying their respects to the dead Israelis. At the end of the service, an official announced the events would continue, saying "The Games must go on."

6

In the Syrian capital of Damascus, it is likely that people strolling down the city's ancient and narrow streets in the late afternoon of September 8, 1972, may have seen a glow on the eastern horizon. What they saw was not a freak desert phenomenon.

Just as evening fell in the Middle East, dozens of Israeli Air Force jets swooped down on El Hameh, a camp on the outskirts of Damascus that housed the headquarters of Al Fatah, the military arm of the Palestine Liberation Organization. Israeli military leaders were convinced that Black September was operating with the sanction of the PLO, and they aimed to make the Palestinians pay for the Olympic murders.

"I hope the Fatah and the Black September movement get the message," said an Israeli Army officer who briefed news reporters shortly after the mission. "But if they don't, we will keep our freedom of action. It will be up to the government of Israel to decide what to do next."

El Hameh wasn't the only Palestinian camp attacked that day. Dozens of Israeli planes hit 10 camps in Syria and Lebanon. More than 200 Palestinian men, women, and children died in the bombings. Three Syrian Air Force planes were shot down when they tried to repel the attack.

It was the largest show of Israeli military force since the Six-Day War. And Israel was far from finished. Eight days later, three columns of Israeli tanks crossed the border into southern Lebanon and leveled dozens of buildings which the Israelis said were housing PLO leaders.

"Our aim is to hit the terrorists as hard as we can to cripple them and to make it clear we mean business," the Israeli military leader told reporters. "The message is directed not only to the terrorists but also to the countries that harbor them."

But military attacks on Palestinian camps were only part of Israel's strategy. High-ranking officials in the Israeli government had another plan for the architects of the Munich massacre.

The Israelis gave a name to their plan.

They called it "Operation Wrath of God."

■　　■　　■

On the morning of September 6, just hours after the Israelis were murdered on the tarmac at Fürstenfeldbruck, 80,000 people gathered in Munich's Olympic Stadium for a memorial service for the dead athletes.

They were addressed by Avery Brundage, head of the International Olympic Committee. A one-time Olympic athlete himself, the 84-year-old Brundage had ruled over the organization that runs the Olympic Games for two decades. Munich would be his last Olympics—Brundage had decided to retire after the 1972 Games.

(continued on page 79)

AVERY BRUNDAGE

Just hours after the murders of the 11 Israeli athletes, Avery Brundage stood in front of a crowd of more than 80,000 people and pledged, "The Games must go on."

Brundage was chairman of the International Olympic Committee (IOC), the organization that oversees the Winter and Summer Olympiads. For two decades, he was the virtual czar of the Olympic Games, ruling over the IOC with a strong will and defiant attitude.

Munich would be his last Olympics; the 84-year-old chairman planned to

Avery Brundage, a former Olympian himself and Chairman of the International Olympic Committee for 20 years, announces the end of the Munich Summer Games. He retired from his post shortly after Munich; the 1972 Olympics were to be his last.

step down from the committee following the 1972 competition.

Brundage was a self-made millionaire. Born in 1887 in Detroit, Michigan, his father was a marginally successful construction company owner. He abandoned his family soon after Avery was born, and the boy was raised by aunts and uncles.

Avery entered the University of Illinois, paying his way through school by working at odd jobs and borrowing from relatives. While a student, Brundage took up sports and found success as a track-and-field competitor—particularly in a competition known as the "all-around."

The all-around was a grueling competition that required the athletes to compete in 10 events in a single day, with only five minutes of rest between events. Brundage was declared national champion in the all-around three times. Today, the all-around has been replaced by the decathlon—10 events staged over a two-day period.

Brundage was a member of the American team that competed in the 1912 Olympics in Stockholm, Sweden, finishing fifth in the five-event pentathlon. The winner of that event was Jim Thorpe, who is still regarded as one of the greatest athletes of the 20th Century.

When Brundage gave up participating in sports he turned his attention to sports administration, helping to found the American Olympic Association, which is now known as the United States Olympic Committee. He also started his own construction company, and soon became head of a successful business that made him rich.

In 1936, Brundage became a member of the International Olympic Committee and, in 1952, its chairman.

One of the earliest controversies in which Brundage found himself was his defense of the 1936 Summer Games in Berlin, Germany. American political leaders felt the United States should protest against Adolf Hitler and the Nazi party by refusing to send a team. But Brundage insisted the United States participate in the Berlin Games.

He said: "The politics of a nation is of no concern to the International Olympic Committee. Nonparticipation would do more harm than good. Hitler would still go on. The Nazis would go on."

History proved him correct. In Berlin, the American team was led by the great black athlete Jesse Owens, who scored important victories and ruined Hitler's plans to showcase the Germans as Olympic champions.

Over the years, Brundage held firm on one rule—no professional athlete would compete in the Olympics.

"Sport is a pastime and a diversion," Brundage said. "The minute it becomes more than that, it's business or work . . . . I suspect that if a professional baseball player discovered one day that he could make more money by going back home and laying bricks for a living he'd go back home and lay bricks . . . . Professional sports should be reported on the entertainment pages along with circuses and vaudeville."

Several times during his administration athletes who were found to have accepted money for competing were disqualified from the Games. In 1947, he forced Canadian figure skater Barbara Ann Scott to return a car given to her by fans or risk expulsion from the 1948 Games.

Once Brundage stepped down, the International Olympic Committee relaxed its rules about professional athletes. Today, stars of professional basketball, hockey, tennis, and other sports regularly compete in the Olympic Games.

Brundage died in 1975 at the age of 87.

(continued from page 76)

"Every civilized person recoils in horror at the barbarous criminal intrusion of terrorists into peaceful Olympic precincts. We mourn our Israeli friends . . . victims of this brutal assault. The Olympic flag and the flags of all the world fly at half mast. Sadly, in this imperfect world, the greater and more important the Olympic Games become, the more they are open to commercial, political, and now criminal pressure."

Brundage had already decided to continue the Games. He told the crowd that the Olympics would be suspended for one day to observe a period of mourning for the dead athletes, but that the competitions would resume.

"The Games must go on," he said.

The Games would go on, but there was no question

they would be played under a somber spirit. The remaining Israeli athletes went home. Shmuel Lalkin, head of the Israeli Olympic Committee, said he disagreed with the decision to continue the Olympics. "They should have called these Games off," he said.

Athletes from Norway, the Philippines, and the Netherlands elected to leave the Games on their own. The governments of Egypt and Syria recalled their teams.

"It just won't be the same thing," said American cyclist John Allis. "The excitement has gone out of the Games. For many of us, the spirit isn't here anymore."

Still, there were many athletic triumphs scored at the 1972 Summer Olympics. In addition to the performances by Mark Spitz and Olga Korbut, other Olympians shone in their events as well.

In track and field, a little-known American named Dave Wottle, who ran while wearing a wrinkled golf cap, won the 800-meter race after starting the contest in last place. Other Americans who became national heroes in the Munich Olympics were boxer Ray Seales, who won the gold medal in the light-heavyweight division, and runner Frank Shorter, who became the first American to win the marathon in 64 years. The marathon is the race of longest duration, often taking its competitors over miles of city streets and country roads.

But not just Americans were scoring important victories. Lasse Viren, a Finn, won two long-distance races, even though he stumbled and fell during one of the competitions. Kenyan Kip Keino won the gold medal in the steeplechase—a race that requires competitors to leap over fences and pools of water—even though he had made his reputation as a long-distance runner and had rarely competed in steeplechase. Australian Shane Gould won three gold medals in women's swimming competitions.

There were disappointments as well—particularly for

American athletes. In track and field, the finals of the men's 100-meter race is regarded as the contest to determine the fastest man on Earth. As the sprinters prepared for the Munich Games, it was clear the competition would come down to three men: Russian Valery Borzov and Americans Eddie Hart and Rey Robinson. But Hart and Robinson never showed up for the finals—their coach had given them the wrong starting time, and when the runners lined up for the 100-meter final, the two Americans were no-shows. Borzov easily won the gold medal. In diving, American Micki King was leading the field going into the last round, but on her dive she slipped and broke her hand. She went home without a medal.

But in no competition did Americans suffer a bigger disappointment than in men's basketball.

In recent years, Olympic rules have permitted NBA stars to compete in the Games, but in 1972 professional athletes were barred. For years, the men's basketball team was composed of college players only. Still, in the entire history of the sport, Americans had never failed to win an Olympic gold medal in basketball.

The 1972 final pitted the Americans against the team from the Soviet Union. With minutes left in the game, the Soviets led by 10 points, but the Americans fought back and with time expiring, American Doug Collins sunk two free throws to put the USA ahead by a score of 51 to 50. The Soviets inbounded the ball to make one final run at the basket, but time expired and the game ended. The Soviets appealed to the referee, claiming they called time out before the final ticks of the clock. The official agreed, and placed three seconds back on the clock. The Soviets tried one more play, missed the basket, and the buzzer sounded. The Americans started celebrating their victory, but the Soviets protested again: they claimed the clock wasn't working correctly. Again, the official restored three seconds to the

Even more drama was unfolding on the basketball floor as the U.S. men's team competed against the U.S.S.R team. Several questionable referee calls and demands by the Soviets resulted in an unfair outcome to the game. The U.S. team refused to accept its second-place silver medals.

clock and gave the Soviets the ball. This time, Russian Alexander Belov took a downcourt pass, knocked two American players out of his way, and sunk a basket at the buzzer. The Soviets were declared the winners.

The American team members bitterly refused to accept their silver medals.

■　　　■　　　■

But while the Americans suffered disappointments in Munich, no team suffered more than the Israelis. The bodies of 10 of the murdered team members were returned to Israel. The victims were given a full state funeral.

When the surviving Israeli athletes stepped off the plane in Tel Aviv, they found a nation in pain. But the athletes who survived the siege seemed to be suffering the greatest anguish.

Tuvia Sokolovsky, who escaped out the back window of Apartment One, said: "I came back to Israel on my own. I lost my best friends . . . . There were five of us and I was the only weightlifter who returned."

Henry Herskowitz, the marksman who carried the Israeli flag in the opening ceremony, escaped from 31 Connollystrasse. Herskowitz had been asleep in Apartment Two, which Moshe Weinberg talked the Palestinians into bypassing.

"We returned to Israel alive and well and the others returned in coffins," he said. "I felt so bad. I saw the rest of the families getting coffins and I felt guilty for being alive. I thought, 'Why do I deserve to be alive while they are back in coffins?'"

The 11th body was that of David Berger, the American who maintained dual nationality. His body was flown to his parents' home in Shaker Heights, Ohio. President Richard M. Nixon dispatched a U.S. Air Force jet to transport Berger's body. More than 800 people attended funeral services for the weightlifter, which were held in Fairmount Temple, the Ohio synagogue Berger attended as a boy.

To many Palestinians, the terrorists who died in the attack were the real heroes. A radio station operating in Egypt known as the Voice of the Palestinian Revolution accused the Munich police of "brutality" and a "thirst for Palestinian blood." The bodies of the five dead terrorists were flown to Libya, where they were buried with the highest honors. More than 30,000 mourners marched in a funeral procession

For David Berger, an American who maintained dual nationality with Israel, the Munich Olympics turned into a battle for his own life and for politics, rather than for a medal. The President of the United States sent an Air Force jet to fly his coffin home to his parents in Ohio.

from Martyrs' Square in the Libyan capital of Tripoli to the nearby Sidi Munaidess Cemetery.

■   ■   ■

Black September was wounded by the Israeli invasions of Lebanon and Syria, but it was not finished. On October 29, a German airliner en route from Damascus to Frankfurt, Germany, was hijacked by two Palestinian terrorists. They told German authorities they would blow up the plane and kill the 17 passengers and crew members unless the Munich police released Jamal Al-Gashey, Adnan Al-Gashey, and Mohammed Safady—the three terrorists who survived the siege at Fürstenfeldbruck.

The German government quickly decided to turn over the terrorists.

"The passengers and crew were threatened with annihilation unless we released the three Palestinian survivors of the Fürstenfeldbruck massacre," said Willie Brandt, the German chancellor. "I then saw no alternative but to yield to this ultimatum and avoid further senseless bloodshed."

The three terrorists had been held in separate German prisons since the Olympic massacre. Jamal Al-Gashey's wounded hand had been bandaged. All three men had been treated well in custody while awaiting their trials. Each man was charged with 11 counts of murder.

The German airliner flew to Zagreb in Yugoslavia to await the arrival of the Palestinians. The terrorists aboard the airliner promised to release the hostages once their three comrades joined them. But they reneged on the deal. Instead of exchanging the passengers and crew of the airliner for the Munich terrorists in Zagreb, the Palestinian hijackers announced that no one would be released until the plane arrived safely in Libya.

The terrorists arrived to an enthusiastic welcome in Libya, and the passengers and crew members were released. In Germany, government leaders breathed a sigh of relief that, at least this time, a tense hostage situation was defused without bloodshed. But in the Middle East, the thousands of Israeli citizens still grieving over the deaths of their athletes seethed with hatred. The three terrorists who survived the attack at Fürstenfeldbruck had gotten away with murder.

And so in Israel, government leaders decided they would take responsibility for hunting down the terrorists as well as the leaders of Black September and make them pay with their lives.

They marked 14 Black September members for death—the three terrorists and 11 others believed to be instrumental in planning the siege on 31 Connollystrasse. The task of hunting down and assassinating the terrorists fell on the Mossad—an arm of the Israeli Defense Force responsible for gathering intelligence and carrying out secret missions. Many countries employ similar units—in America, the Central Intelligence Agency is responsible for gathering intelligence on foreign governments considered unfriendly to the United States.

The Mossad struck first at Wael Zwaiter, a terrorist leader in Europe and the cousin of Yasir Arafat, head of the Palestine Liberation Organization. The Mossad found Zwaiter living openly in Rome, taking few precautions to safeguard his life considering the Israeli attacks that had been launched on Palestinian camps just after the massacre.

Mossad agents watched Zwaiter for several days, then struck as he entered the lobby of his Rome apartment building. Two agents walked up to Zwaiter in the lobby and shot him 14 times.

Mahmoud Hamsari was next. He was regarded as one of the planners of the Connollystrasse attack. He was also living in Rome. Mossad agents placed a bomb in his apartment and detonated it on December 8, 1972.

Three Black September leaders were killed in Beirut, Lebanon, in the spring of 1973. One of the Mossad agents assigned to the operation was Ehud Barak, who would have led the commando raid at Fürstenfeldbruck had the Germans agreed to turn the rescue over to the Israelis. This time, Barak's mission was much more covert. He dressed in women's clothes and a wig, and walked down a Beirut street with his arm around the waist of agent Muki Betser, who was posing as Barak's "boyfriend." Barak carried two hand grenades hidden in his bra. The target was Abu Yussuf, a PLO leader.

In their disguises, the two Mossad agents attracted little notice as they made their way through Beirut streets, finally finding Yussuf's apartment. Suddenly, they burst through the door with machine guns blazing, killing the PLO leader, his wife, and three bodyguards. Similar operations

Ehud Barak, a commando who assassinated Black September leaders after Munich, eventually left the military and rose in politics to become Prime Minister. He became more liberal, seeking compromise with Palestinians. Barak was voted out of office in 2001 by Israeli citizens fearful for their safety.

by agents in Beirut wiped out two more of the targets on the Mossad's list.

But the Mossad botched some missions and innocent people died. In July 1973, Mossad agents thought they had tracked down Black September leader Ali Hassan Salameh in Lillehammer, Norway. Mossad agents shot the man as he got off a bus with his wife near his Lillehammer apartment.

The victim was not Salameh. It was Ahmed Bouchiki, a Moroccan man working as a waiter at a Lillehammer restaurant. What's more, the two Mossad agents who shot Bouchiki were arrested after police spotted their getaway car on a Lillehammer street, and three others were apprehended before they had a chance to leave the country. All the Mossad agents were convicted of Bouchiki's murder, but all five were quietly released from Norwegian prisons less than two years later.

Still, the Mossad remained committed to its mission. In 1973, the covert agency delivered what may have been the knockout blow to Black September when some 40 Israeli commandos made an amphibious raid on a Beirut beach, targeting Black September leaders Kamal Nasser and Kemel Adwan. The commandos killed more than 100 PLO guerillas in the raid, including Nasser and Adwan.

Over the years the Mossad kept on the trail of Black September, eventually eliminating all but two of the names on its list. Jamal Al-Gashey, one of the Munich terrorists, and Abu Daoud, who helped plan the siege on 31 Connollystrasse, survived Operation Wrath of God.

Al-Gashey has spent the years since Munich in hiding. After arriving in Libya aboard the hijacked Lufthansa plane, Al-Gashey has lived in the Arab world under an assumed name.

He told a reporter that he harbors no regrets about his role in the murders.

"My family has paid a big price, but we think it is the price that every Palestinian family has to pay to get what it deserves," he said.

Abu Daoud was arrested in Jordan about a year after the Munich attack while planning a siege on the U.S. Embassy in Amman, the Jordanian capital. Daoud escaped a death sentence when, in a show of good will to the Palestinian people, King Hussein granted him a pardon. He spent years hiding deep in the Arab world, finding sanctuary in Tunisia and Algeria, and also

traveling in eastern Europe. The Mossad caught up with him in 1981 in Poland where an Israeli assassin shot him five times, but Daoud survived the attack.

Following the assassination attempt Daoud slipped back into the West Bank and, in fact, became a member of the Palestinian Authority—the governing body elected to oversee the transition of the Israeli-occupied territories into a Palestinian nation. Over the years, his resolve to eliminate Israel softened, and he became a voice of moderation in the Palestinian Authority—twice voting for a resolution that recognizes Israel's right to exist as a country.

"I voted on the side of peace," said Daoud.

Israel would never forget his role in the massacre. Nor would Germany. In 1999, the Munich police issued an arrest warrant for Daoud, but authorities have been unable to take him into custody because he remains safely out of German jurisdiction in his West Bank home.

Abu Daoud, one of the terrorists who took the Israelis hostage, in a 1977 photo. He was captured in Jordan in 1973 but was released by the king in a show of good will. Daoud survived a later assassination attempt and eventually became a moderating leader and force in the Arab war against Israel.

President Clinton led talks during the 1993 Middle East peace accords. Israeli Prime Minister Yitzhak Rabin and Palestinian leader Yasir Arafat signed an agreement to withdraw Israeli forces from designated Palestinian areas. Eventual Arab self-rule is the elusive, ultimate goal of continued negotiations.

The Holy Martyrs

J ust past dawn on May 7, 2001, an Israeli surveillance plane patrolling the eastern Mediterranean Sea spotted a Lebanese fishing vessel. Although it is not unusual to find fishing boats in that part of the Mediterranean, the Israeli pilot grew suspicious because this craft seemed to be doing no fishing.

Israeli gun ships were quickly called in. They surrounded the Lebanese boat, named the Santorini, and boarded her. The crew put up no resistance.

The Israelis soon uncovered a cache of guns, ammunition, and explosives. Among the weapons found aboard the Santorini were SA-7 Strella missiles—small projectiles fired from a shoulder-mounted weapon. After questioning the crew members, the Israelis learned the arms were to be delivered to the Popular Front for the Liberation of Palestine, one of several extremist groups operating in the Middle East.

Ahmed Jibril, head of the Popular Front, quickly claimed ownership of the weapons. In fact, Jibril said that while the Israelis may have captured the weapons aboard the Santorini, they had missed three earlier shipments.

There was no question the Israelis were concerned about the continuing ability of terrorists to obtain destructive weapons.

"The SA-7 can take down a Boeing 747," Yedidia Ya'ari, commander of Israel's navy, told reporters.

Indeed, three decades after Munich, the Middle East teeters on the edge of war despite the best efforts of many Palestinians and Israelis to put the Olympic massacre behind them and find a lasting peace.

On September 13, 1993, Israeli Prime Minster Yitzhak Rabin and Palestine Liberation Organization leader Yasir Arafat extended their hands to one another in peace. Just moments before, Arafat and Rabin had signed the "Declaration of Principles," providing a framework for how Israel planned to withdraw its troops from the occupied West Bank and other territories, making way for Palestinian self-government.

The agreement was brokered by U.S. President Bill Clinton, who urged the two longtime enemies to join hands. Standing on the South Lawn of the White House in Washington, Arafat extended his hand to Rabin, who accepted it.

Rabin said: "We the soldiers who have returned from the battle stained with blood, we who have fought against you, the Palestinians, we say to you today in a loud and clear voice: 'Enough of blood and tears! Enough!'"

For 21 years after the Olympic massacre, the Israelis and Palestinians had waged war on each other, often drawing other nations into the conflict. In 1973, Israel fought off attacks by Egypt and Syria to regain their territories lost in the Six-Day War. The attacks were

launched during Yom Kippur, the holiest day on the Jewish calendar, and the conflict came to be known as the Yom Kippur War. Again, the Israelis defeated the Arab states, but Israel suffered heavy losses and did not score the type of overwhelming victory it had enjoyed in 1967.

In 1977 Egyptian President Anwar Sadat shocked his Arab allies by making an overture of peace toward Israel. Two years later, Sadat and Israeli Prime Minister Menachem Begin signed a peace treaty in Washington.

The treaty proved to be unpopular in the Arab world, where an Islamic fundamentalist movement was sweeping through the Middle East. In Iran, Muslim clerics under Ayatollah Ruhollah Khomeini had taken power, aiming to discard western influences and marking for death any leader who sought accommodation with Israel or its allies, including the United States. In 1979, Sadat was assassinated by Muslim fundamentalists.

In May 2001, an Israeli surveillance plane saw a suspicious fishing boat that was later boarded and found to be full of weapons en route to a Palestinian extremist group. Such incidents prove that the war between Palestinians and Israelis is clearly not resolved, regardless of decades of valiant effort on both sides.

Relations between the Palestinians and Israelis remained bitter, but as the years dragged on both sides grew weary of the constant attacks and counterattacks. When Rabin came to power in 1991, he opened peace talks with Arafat.

"You know, we have a lot of work to do," Rabin told Arafat during the signing of the peace accords in 1993.

"I know and I am prepared to do my part," Arafat answered.

■   ■   ■

The Germans had named the Munich Olympiad "The Games of Peace and Joy." Their intent was to introduce the "New Germany" to the world—to rid the nation of its Nazi past. But after the Munich massacre, many Germans questioned whether the Games had served that purpose.

Shortly after the Games ended, the German newspaper Süddeutsche Zeitung wrote: "There may not exist a great city whose people are less imperialistic, less aggressive, more peaceable, more full of simple human qualities than those of the Bavarian metropolis. However, various slogans have stuck to the name 'Munich.' Capital of the (Nazi) movement. Originator of politically ideological lawlessness. Site of the capitulation of the law before naked power. 'Brown' Munich. Bulwark of vengeance. However contourless and emotional these notions have seemed to us, they now appear to be confirmed."

■   ■   ■

The Olympic Games survived Munich. When the Israeli team arrived in Montreal, Canada, for the 1976 Summer Games, the athletes found a decidedly different attitude toward security than the Germans had exhibited four years before. The Canadian government made security in the Olympic Village a paramount consideration, particularly for the Israeli team. Dozens of officers from the Royal Canadian Mounted Police were assigned to protect the Israeli athletes for the two weeks they spent in Montreal; indeed, the athletes' apartments in the Olympic Village were guarded 24 hours a day by officers from the elite national police force of Canada.

The Israeli team marched into Montreal's Olympic Stadium along with the other nations competing in the 1976 Summer Games. Selected to carry the flag for the Israeli team was track star Esther Shahamorov, a survivor of the Munich siege. This time she made it to the finals in her event, finishing sixth overall.

The Canadians had nothing to fear from Black September or any other terrorist group—no security incidents marred the Montreal Games.

But the sponsors of future Olympiads were not so lucky. In America during the 1990s, the so-called "militia" movement gained fervor among people who were convinced their government was secretly conspiring to deny them rights that were guaranteed under the U.S. Constitution, particularly the right to carry guns. Some of the militia members advocated armed conflict and even terrorism aimed at the federal government. Oklahoma City bomber Timothy McVeigh was inspired by the militia movement.

So was Eric Robert Rudolph, a 28-year-old handyman from the rugged hills of North Carolina.

In 1996, the Summer Games arrived in Atlanta, Georgia. On July 27, the ninth day of the Games, thousands of people gathered in Centennial Olympic Park in Atlanta for a free concert. Suddenly, a bomb exploded in the park, injuring more than 100 people and killing one woman— Alice Hawthorne, a mother from Albany, Georgia.

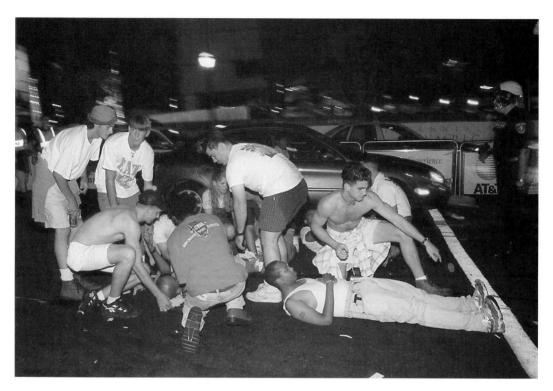

Terrorism and bombings are not restricted to the Middle East. Americans were shocked when a blast rocked a popular, crowded park at the 1996 Atlanta, Georgia Olympics. In this picture, spectators come to the aid of those injured in the attack.

After the blast, investigators found the remnants of the device that killed Hawthorne—it was a crudely-made pipe bomb that had been hidden in a backpack left near the Olympic Park stage.

Months later, two more bombs exploded in the Atlanta area, damaging an abortion clinic and a nightclub frequented by gay people. No one was injured in the blasts.

For two years, police scrambled for leads in the bombings. But in January 1998, a security guard was killed and a nurse injured when a bomb exploded at an abortion clinic in Birmingham, Alabama. A witness had seen a pickup truck near the blast site and took down the license plate number. That led police to Rudolph. After interviewing people near Rudolph's home in Nantahala, North Carolina, police determined that he may have been a member of the "Christian Identity" cult whose members believe the white race is

God's chosen. Cult members are suspicious of the government's intentions and harbor hatreds against blacks, Jews, and homosexuals. Christian Identity members are also militantly opposed to abortion.

On October 14, 1998, Rudolph was named as a suspect in all four bombings.

"The fatal bombing in Atlanta was a terrorist attack aimed at thousands of innocent persons gathered at the Olympic Park," said Federal Bureau of Investigation (FBI) Director Louis Freeh. "Within the FBI's Domestic Terrorism Program, there is no higher priority than the capture of Eric Robert Rudolph."

During their investigation, police learned that two months before the Olympic bombing, Rudolph sold his home and stopped seeing family and friends. He also started using the alias "Bob Randolph."

Police threw out a dragnet for Rudolph, who had apparently disappeared into the North Carolina hills. Soon, they found his truck mired in the mud about eight miles from a trailer he was known to have rented. In a storage shed near the trailer, federal investigators found nails similar to the nails packed into the shrapnel charge that exploded in Olympic Park. What's more, the steel used to form the pipe bomb in Atlanta was traced to a metal factory in Franklin, near Rudolph's Nantahala home. Also, police learned, a friend of Rudolph's worked in the factory.

FBI agents continued their search for the suspected Olympic bomber. They traipsed through the Nantahala National Forest, but soon determined that the foliage was so thick that Rudolph could easily evade their manhunt. They remain convinced he is hiding in the North Carolina hills, where he may be receiving food and other aid from Christian Identity cult members.

"We would hope that nobody would look at this defendant . . . as a hero," Louis Freeh said.

By July 1998 Eric Rudolph had made the FBI's Ten Most-Wanted List.

He remains at large.

■   ■   ■

The Israelis and Palestinians have never been able to build on the peace movement that Rabin and Arafat started with their handshake in 1993. Both sides never got over their suspicions of each other, and both sides also found themselves fending off radical elements in their own countries that were very much opposed to making concessions in the name of peace.

In Israel, many Jews remained in fear that once they turned over the West Bank and other territories, they would lose the protection against Arab aggression they had enjoyed since the Six-Day War. Some Jews turned to terrorism themselves to prevent the establishment of a Palestinian homeland.

On November 4, 1995, Yigal Amir, a 24-year-old Israeli law student, attended a peace rally where Rabin was scheduled to speak. At the rally, Amir drew a 9-mm Beretta handgun and assassinated the prime minister.

He was sentenced to life in prison. He spends his days reading the Talmud—the book of ancient Jewish laws—and answering mail he receives from teenage girls, strangely smitten with the handsome assassin.

Amir remains convinced that Rabin's peace initiative would have endangered the Israelis, and the only way to stall the return of the Palestinians was to murder the prime minister.

"If I hadn't (killed Rabin), there would have been a Palestinian state for awhile already," Amir told a reporter in 1999. "We would have lost everything."

Following the assassination of Rabin, other Israeli

Rabin's signing of the 1993 peace agreement turned out to be his death sentence. Two years later, Yigal Amir, a conservative Jew, killed Rabin because he thought such peace initiatives would mean the end of the Israeli state and Jewish homeland.

leaders struggled with the peace process. One of them was Ehud Barak, the former Israeli commando who had assassinated Black September leaders in the aftermath of Munich. After a career in the military, Barak entered Israeli politics. As prime minister, the former commander was considered a moderate, willing to make concessions to the Palestinians. But as terrorist attacks on Israelis continued, citizens of Israel grew concerned for their safety and demanded a stronger hand in dealing with the Palestinians. In Israeli elections in early 2001, voters ousted Barak and turned to Ariel Sharon, a former military commander who pledged to answer terrorist attacks quickly and ruthlessly.

As for Arafat, the Palestinian leader has never been able to shake the suspicion harbored by Israelis that he took a personal hand in authorizing the siege on 31 Connollystrasse.

In fact, in 1999 Abu Daoud linked Arafat directly to the Munich massacre. Abu Daoud's biography, *Palestine: From Jerusalem to Munich,* which was published in France, said that the Palestinian leader was briefed on the plans for the Olympic attack before the terrorists were dispatched to Germany. Shortly before carrying out the siege, Daoud said, he met with Arafat who wished him success.

"Allah protect you," Arafat told Daoud.

Meanwhile, it became increasingly clear that Arafat no longer controlled the radical Palestinians who still aimed to make war on Israel. Many Palestinians joined terrorist groups that advocate Islamic fundamentalism. Two groups that are of most concern to Israelis are Hamas and Islamic Jihad, organizations that use suicide bombers—known as shaheed or "holy martyrs"—to commit terrorism. Jihad is an Arab word for "holy war."

On June 1, 2001, a Hamas terrorist armed with a bomb blew himself up outside a disco in Tel Aviv, killing 22 people and injuring hundreds. Israel retaliated with an air strike on Hamas headquarters in the West Bank, killing six Palestinian leaders and two children walking on the street outside the building. One of the Hamas leaders killed in the strike was Jamal Mansour, whom Israelis claimed had planned the disco murders. Israeli leaders insisted the Hamas terrorists were planning similar attacks.

Just a few months later, Hamas struck again—a suicide

bomber killed 14 people outside a pizza restaurant in Jerusalem. Again, Israel responded with air strikes against Hamas strongholds.

"Anyone who thinks that the war against terrorism is a Ping-Pong war simply does not understand it," Israeli cabinet member Ephraim Sneh said shortly after the air strike. "You must also make preemptive strikes. As soon as you know about terrorists preparing an attack it is your duty to strike first."

Still, members of Hamas and Islamic Jihad believe Shari'a—Islamic religious law—provides for the use of martyrs in the waging of the jihad.

"All children who are born eventually die," said West Bank terrorist leader Abdullah Shami. "And death is painful, except in the case of martyrs, who feel no pain as they commit the act that leads to their martyrdom. . . . Our bodies are the only weapons we have."

Two teenaged sisters, Yulia and Yelena Nelimov, died in June 2001 when a suicide bomber set off explosives at a disco in an Israeli city. The bomber killed 19 and injured more than 90 people. Such acts of terrorism have sadly become part of daily life in this country.

Chronology

1945   World War II ends; many Jews displaced by the war make their way to Palestine in the Middle East.

1947   Fighting breaks out between Jewish settlers in the British colony of Palestine and armies of the Arab states, touching off the Israeli War of Independence.

1948   The nation of Israel declares its independence. Arabs and Israelis agree to a truce ending Israel's War of Independence; thousands of Palestinian Arabs are forced to live in refugee camps.

1950   Legislature of Israel adopts "Law of Return" recognizing the right of all Jews to emigrate to Israel.

1964   Palestine Liberation Organization formed.

1967   Israel wins the Six-Day War, driving armies of Syria, Egypt, and Jordan away from its borders. Israel captures territory from those countries, forcing Palestinians to flee to refugee camps. In the camps, Palestinians begin waging a war of terrorism on Israel.

1970   In September, King Hussein of Jordan drives Palestinians from refugee camps in his country; Hussein's campaign against the refugees comes to be known as "Black September," a name that will be adopted by a Palestinian terrorist organization.

1971   Black September terrorists murder Jordanian Prime Minister Wasif Tell.

1972   *May:* Four Black September terrorists hijack a Sabena Airlines plane; two are killed when Israeli commandos storm the plane and free the hostages.

1972   *August 26:* Summer Olympic Games commence in Munich, Germany.

1972   *September 5:* Eight Black September terrorists sneak into the Olympic Village in Munich, kill two Israeli athletes and take nine others hostage; that night, five of the terrorists and all nine hostages die in a shootout at an airport near Munich.

1972   *September 8:* In retaliation for the Munich massacre, Israeli Air Force planes attack 10 refugee camps in Syria and Lebanon, killing more than 200 Palestinians.

Chronology

1972   *October 29:* Black September terrorists hijack a German airliner, demanding the release of the three terrorists who survived the Munich raid. German officials agree to their demands. Israel responds by marking 14 Black September terrorists and leaders for death; all but two of the Palestinians on the list are eventually assassinated by Israeli agents.

1979   Egyptian President Anwar Sadat signs a peace treaty with Israel.

1993   Israel Prime Minister Yitzhak Rabin and PLO leader Yasir Arafat sign a peace accord establishing principles for a Palestinian homeland.

1995   Rabin is assassinated by Israeli Yigal Amir, one of many Israelis opposed to peace with the Palestinians.

1996   Bomb explodes in Centennial Olympic Park in Atlanta, Georgia, during the Summer Games and kills a woman; right-wing extremist Eric Robert Rudolph emerges as a suspect.

2001   Palestinian suicide bomber kills 22 people at a disco in the Israeli city of Tel Aviv; it is one of many attacks launched by two Palestinian terrorist organizations—Hamas and Islamic Jihad.

Bibliography

Blumenfeld, Laura. "Slain Leader's Legacy Lives on, Assassin Admits." *The Washington Post,* May 14, 1999.

Calahan, Alexander B. "Countering Terrorism: The Israeli Response to the 1972 Munich Olympic Massacre and the Development of Independent Covert Action Teams." Thesis prepared for the Marine Corps Command and Staff College, April 1995.

Denby, David. "No Rules—New Interpretations of the Massacre at the Munich Olympcs." *The New Yorker,* Aug. 21-28, 2000.

Finder, Chuck. "HBO Documentary Relives Tragedy at the 1972 Munich Olympics." *Pittsburgh Post-Gazette,* Sept. 12, 2000.

Friedman, Thomas. "Rabin and Arafat Seal Their Accord as Clinton Applauds 'Brave Gamble.'" *The New York Times,* Sept. 14, 1993.

Goldberg, Jeffrey. "Letter from Gaza: The Martyr Strategy." *The New Yorker,* July 9, 2001.

Goodale, Gloria. "New Views of the Tragedy of the '72 Munich Olympics." *The Christian Science Monitor,* Sept. 8, 2000.

Goodenough, Patrick. "Munich Olympics Massacre Said to be PLO Operation." Conservative News Service, May 5, 1999.

Goodenough, Patrick. "Ohio Congressman wants Terrorist Extradited to United States." Conservative News Service, June 21, 1999.

Groussard, Serge. *The Blood of Israel, the Massacre of the Israeli Athletes.* New York: William Morrow and Co. Inc., 1975.

Kraft, Dina. "Pain of Munich Massacre Still Vivid 25 Years Later." The Associated Press, Aug. 31, 1997.

Litsky, Frank. "Avery Brundage of Olympics Dies." *The New York Times,* May 9, 1975.

LoLordo, Ann. "Abu Daoud Tells All About His Role in Munich Operation." *The Star,* July 1, 1999.

Bibliography

Marcovitz, Hal. *Terrorism.* Philadelphia: Chelsea House Publishers, 2001.

McKay, Jim. *The Real McKay, My Wide World of Sports.* New York: Dutton, 1998.

Murphey, Frances B. "Memories of Olympians from Northeast Ohio." *Akron Beacon Journal,* Feb. 8, 1998.

Nash, Jay Robert. *Terrorism in the 20th Century.* New York: M. Evans and Co. Inc., 1998.

Reeve, Simon. *One Day in September.* New York: Arcade Publishing, 2000.

Shuster, Alvin. "Despicable Act Decried at Arena Rites." *The New York Times,* Sept. 7, 1972.

Smith, Red. "Flame Glows Amid Pageantry." *The New York Times,* Aug. 27, 1972.

Smith, Terence. "Scores of Israeli Planes Strike 10 Guerrilla Bases in a Reprisal for Munich." *The New York Times,* Sept. 9, 1972.

Tarabay, Jamie. "Israelis Raid Hamas Site, Killing Eight." The Associated Press, Aug. 1, 2001.

Yeomans, Patricia Henry. *An Approved History of the Olympic Games.* Sherman Oaks, Calif.: Alfred Publishing Co., 1984.

"An Immigrant from America." *Life,* Sept. 15, 1972.

"Eric Rudolph Charged in Olympic Park Bombing." FBI News Release, Oct. 14, 1998.

"Horror and Death at the Olympics." *Time,* Sept. 18, 1972.

"Israel Imposes Life Sentences on 2 Arab Women Hijackers." *The New York Times,* Aug. 15, 1972.

"Israeli Team had 18 Athletes and Coaches." United Press International, Sept. 6, 1972.

Bibliography

"Olympic Village Starts to Look Like Home to Athletes." The Associated Press, Aug. 12, 1972.

"Rudolph Now Faces Olympic Bombing Charges." The Associated Press, Oct. 15, 1998.

"Slain Athlete is Buried in His Home Town of Cleveland." *The New York Times,* Sept. 9, 1972.

World Wide Web

Munich Remembered: 1972 Attack Led to Increased Security
http://www.CNN.com

Munich's Intricately Tented Olympic Venue was an Architectural Masterpiece
http://cbc.ca/olympics/05_history/1972.html

The Role of the Military in Israel
http://www.jajz-ed.org.il/juice/2000/israeli_society/is9.html

The 1948 War
http://www.us-israel.org/jsource/History/1948_War.html

U.S. Citizenship and Dual Nationality
http://travel.state.gov/loss.html
http://travel.state.gov/dualnationality.html

Further Reading

Groussard, Serge. *The Blood of Israel, the Massacre of the Israeli Athletes.* New York: William Morrow and Co. Inc., 1975.

Marcovitz, Hal. *Terrorism.* Philadelphia: Chelsea House Publishers, 2001.

McKay, Jim. *The Real McKay, My Wide World of Sports.* New York: Dutton, 1998.

Nash, Jay Robert. *Terrorism in the 20th Century.* New York: M. Evans and Co. Inc., 1998.

Reeve, Simon. *One Day in September.* New York: Arcade Publishing, 2000.

Yeomans, Patricia Henry. *An Approved History of the Olympic Games.* Sherman Oaks, Calif.: Alfred Publishing Co., 1984.

Index

Index

Index

Picture Credits

Cover Photo: Associated Press, AP

HAL MARCOVITZ is a journalist for *The Morning Call,* a newspaper based in Allentown, Pennsylvania. He has written more than 25 books for young readers. He lives in Chalfont, Pennsylvania, with his wife Gail, and daughters Ashley and Michelle.

JILL McCAFFREY has served for four years as national chairman of the Armed Forces Emergency Services of the American Red Cross. Ms. McCaffrey also serves on the board of directors for Knollwood—the Army Distaff Hall. The former Jill Ann Faulkner, a Massachusetts native, is the wife of Barry R. McCaffrey, who served in President Bill Clinton's cabinet as director of the White House Office of National Drug Control Policy. The McCaffreys are the parents of three grown children: Sean, a major in the U.S. Army; Tara, an intensive care nurse and captain in the National Guard; and Amy, a seventh grade teacher. The McCaffreys also have two grandchildren, Michael and Jack.